MIRACULOUS MIRROR

A JOURNEY OF SELF-DISCOVERY AND PURPOSE SEEKING

NORMAN CHIMEZIE FLETCHER

Zoba's Facilities

ISBN: 978-978-782-718-5 (e-book)

First Edition: September 2023

Published by Zoba's Facilities in Nigeria

https://zobasfacilities.com

Email: zobasfacilities@gmail.com

Tel: 2348080887542

DEDICATION

To my daughter, the light of my life.

To my sons, who fill my heart with joy every moment of the day.

To my children, wife, and family, my whole heart living outside my body, who continue to inspire me to tell stories that matter and are impactful.

To the person I was writing this book, and the person I am now by privilege, an ordained Pastor of the Church of Christ.

To the ones reading this, thank you for giving my words a chance. May you find the courage, joy, and love contained within these pages.

Contents

CHAPTER ONE: MIRRORS

All of us have been around mirrors our whole life and we can take for granted what a useful tool a mirror is. It shows our face exactly how it is at the moment we look into it, so that we may make what corrections we can. I know there are a few vain people who mainly use a mirror to stare at their perceived beauty, but for most of us, a mirror is a tool we use to make corrections—checking to see if we have removed all dirt after having washed our face, shaving, and fixing our hair.

A mirror is not like a photograph, which captures our likeness at a specific moment in time, and as time passes the picture stays the same. We are changing, and over time, the picture may no longer reflect how we look anymore.

With Photoshop and other software, we can now change a picture of our face to make it look the way we wish it looked, and not how we actually do look.

But a mirror is not that way. It reveals the way we look at the present moment without any dishonesty. It shows us what is truly there. The mirror is not trying to hurt our feelings or make us feel good or bad, it just reflects what is there. The mirror shows us our natural face, our true face. The mirror will reveal every dirty spot and smudge, every mole and wrinkle, every receding hairline or hair on our face that needs to be removed.

Mirrors are all around us, even on our smartphones. They complement us when we look good and provide a stark reality check when we don't. They've become essential in many aspects of life, such as driving a car, and they've been part of man's experience for thousands of years.

According to the website, Mirror History, the genesis of the reflective instrument is probably in nature: people noticed their reflection in the water and were entranced. For many people, the feeling that Narcissus experienced had to be replicated, so some genius began polishing different kinds of stone until a reflection appeared. A "natural" for this, which didn't need much polishing, is obsidian—black volcanic glass.

"Some examples of this kind of mirrors have been found in Turkey dating back at least 6000 years," Mirror History says. It continues:

The Ancient Egyptians used polished copper to produce mirrors, and often the round face of the mirror would be embellished with ornamentation. The Ancient Mesopotamians also produced polished metal mirrors and mirrors made from polished stone were known in Central and South America from about 2000 BC. In China, mirrors began to be made from metal alloys, a mixture of tin and copper called speculum metal that could be highly polished to make a reflective surface as well as mirrors made of polished bronze. Metal alloys or precious metals mirrors were very valuable items in ancient times and only affordable to the very wealthy.

It is believed that mirrors made of metal-backed glass were first produced in Lebanon in the first century A.D., and the Romans made crude mirrors from blown glass with lead backings, the website says.

In the Bible, mirrors are referenced as early as the eighth century B.C. Book of Proverbs. *"Can you, with Him, spread out the skies, Strong as a molten mirror?"* asks Elihu of his famously afflicted friend in Job 37:18.

Other examples from the Holy Scripture include:

Exodus 38:8 NASB *"Moreover, he made the laver of bronze with its base of bronze, from the mirrors of the serving women who served at the doorway of the tent of meeting."*

Isaiah 3:23 NASB *"… hand mirrors, undergarments, turbans and veils."*

Proverbs 27:19 NASB *"As in water face reflects face, so the heart of man reflects man."*

James 1:23–24 NASB *"For if anyone is a hearer of the word and not a doer, he is like a man who looks at his natural face in a mirror, for once he has looked at himself and gone away, he has immediately forgotten what kind of person he was."*

2 Corinthians 3:18 NASB *"But we all, with unveiled face, beholding as in a mirror the glory of the Lord, are being transformed into the same image from glory to glory, just as from the Lord, the Spirit."*

But perhaps the best-known verse from the Bible that refers to mirrors is 1 Corinthians 13:12 NASB *"For now we see in a mirror dimly, but then face to face; now I know in part, but then I will know fully just as I also have been fully known."*

One notable thing about the references to mirrors in the Bible, though, is the absence of any sense of supernatural powers. Superstitions surrounding mirrors have captivated man over the ages, and the thought that breaking a mirror results in seven years of bad luck persists to this day. That idea comes from an old Roman legend that a soul shatters with a broken mirror and it takes seven years to regenerate it.

In addition, in some cultures, mirrors are covered when someone dies, because, as the superstition goes, a mirror can trap the soul of the person who dies.

"It is also said that a mirror in the house falling from a wall is a sign that someone was going to die," Mirror History says.

If anything, we might look at the entire Bible itself as a mirror. As with any great literature, when we read Scripture, contemplating its characters, stories, and lessons, we see our own lives more clearly.

The Word of God is like a mirror that shows us our spiritual self, our inner man, which we could not see otherwise. The Word of God, this mirror to our soul, flatters no man! It reveals to us our sins and how we have missed the mark.

Without the mirror of the Word of God, we can fancy ourselves as quite spiritually beautiful. We may fancy ourselves as spiritually attractive, especially as we compare ourselves to others, we deem far less spiritual than we are.

As we hear the Word of God and look into the mirror of the Word of God, we see ourselves as we are at that moment. Not spiritually beautiful or handsome, but in need of a makeover.

God's Word lays bare our soul when we hear it, when we read it, and when we meditate on it. It shows us every ugly wart and wrinkle of who we are on the inside. The Word of God shows us our ugliness so that we will correct it and be made spiritually beautiful in that area of our life.

In James 1:23–24, the problem is not the Word of God, because God's Word is perfect in every way, and it will show us who we are if we have eyes to see and ears to hear. The problem is with the person who is a hearer only and not a doer. They are like the person who looks into the mirror and sees what needs to be changed and they do nothing about it. They leave Sunday service having heard the Word of God and having understood what God revealed to them about themselves but did nothing. They may have felt a sense of conviction or remorse, they may even have cried or been pierced to the heart; but here is the problem: they do not respond in repentance and with a commitment to consistent obedience. They have no desire to change.

They hear the Word in Sunday service, and because they have no desire to repent, no desire to change, by Sunday evening or by Monday, whatever the mirror of God's work had revealed to them about the sin in their life has been forgotten. It is gone from their mind.

If anyone calls themselves a Christian, if anyone here believes themselves to be a follower of Christ and does not respond to the Word of God in repentance and obedience, you are deceiving yourself, as James said in verse 22. You have grossly miscalculated what it means to be saved by the very blood of Christ and what it means to be a follower of Jesus our Lord.

Jesus said to His followers, and He says to anyone here today to which this applies:

Luke 6:46 NASB *"Why do you call Me, 'Lord, Lord,' and do not do what I say?"*

Jesus asked this question because to call Jesus "Lord," to profess Christ as Lord and Savior, yet to have no desire to obey Him, is inconsistent with calling Him "Lord." The two do not match. You cannot call Him your Lord and then turn around and ignore what His Word says to you.

Jesus makes this point in the most forceful of terms here:

John 3:36 NASB *"He who believes in the Son has eternal life; but he who does not obey the Son will not see life, but the wrath of God abides on him."*

These are the words of the only one who can provide eternal life through His sacrificial death and glorious resurrection. He has said that the one who does not obey Him will not see life.

The pattern of life for anyone who has been saved by Christ is to consistently obey Him, because we have been converted from an open and active rebellion against God to sonship and friendship, and we have come under His lordship.

John 15:14 NASB *"You are My friends if you do what I command you."*

1 John 2:3–4 NASB *"By this we know that we have come to know Him, if we keep His commandments. The one who says, "I have come to know Him," and does not keep His commandments, is a liar, and the truth is not in him."*

Will you and I follow Jesus and the Word of God perfectly? No. Can we have an attitude of rebellion at times? Absolutely. But the tenor and tone of our life, if we are His sheep, must be to follow our shepherd!

If we hear the Word of God and it reveals to us the sin in our life, and the areas that need to be addressed, and we ignore what the Word of God has revealed to us about ourselves, then we are like the man who looks at his face in the mirror and sees he needs to shave, but does nothing about it, and he walks away from the mirror and quickly forgets that his face is unkempt and in need of a shave. Or the woman who looks at her face in the mirror and sees she has some rollers she needs to take out of her hair and does nothing about it, and she walks away from the mirror and quickly forgets that she still has rollers in her hair.

Just like the man and the women who ignored, then forgot about what they saw in the mirror, and everywhere they went, everyone else saw what they should have taken care of but did not. In the same way, when the Word of God reveals sin in our life to us and we ignore it, do nothing about it, and quickly forget it, the tragedy is that the sin is still there, and we suffer for it. Those around us who see that sin and are very often affected by it, are hurt by it. Those around us are hurt by our unkind words or acts of selfishness, unfaithfulness, violent outbursts, or fill-in-the-blank on how our sin that God has shown, and we did not address hurts those who we love, and it hurts us as well.

Please know that if you are a son or daughter of God, He will not leave you in this condition. He will not let you be content with just hearing the Word and not addressing the sin He is making you aware of. If you do not respond in repentance and obedience, you will receive the discipline and correction of the Lord.

Hebrews 12:6 NLT *"The Lord disciplines those He loves."*

Hebrews 12:11 NASB *"All discipline for the moment seems not to be joyful, but sorrowful; yet to those who have been trained by it, afterwards it yields the peaceful fruit of righteousness."*

How about just responding in repentance and obedience today instead of going through the discipline of the Lord, which can seem so sorrowful? How about repenting and obeying today and enjoying the fruit of righteousness?

James has given us a picture of what it looks like to respond rightly to hearing the Word of God.

James 1:25 NASB *"But one who looks intently at the perfect law, the law of liberty, and abides by it, not having become a forgetful hearer but an effectual doer, this man will be blessed in what he does."*

James tells us if we are going to be doers of the Word of God, it starts with our attitude toward hearing the Word.

As believers, are we coming to church on Sunday and to our daily time of meeting with God through prayer and study of His Word with a desire to hear and understand everything God has to say to us about Himself and us? Are we listening intently to the Word being preached, humbling ourselves so we can peer into the Word and what is being said so that that we may apply God's Word to our hearts? When the Word is preached or taught and you are shown your sin in the mirror of God's perfect law, do you repent immediately, on the spot, not waiting until later to address it? Are you coming to His Word with a sincere desire to be shown your ugliness so you can confess it to God and cry out for His forgiveness, mercy, and grace so that you can be changed by the power of His Word and His Spirit?

Loving obedience has always been what God requires. Starting with Adam and throughout the

Old Testament and New Testament, God wants a people for Himself who will follow Him. Obedience starts with choosing to obey.

Psalm 119 expresses this firm commitment that we as believers must have every time, we hear His Word. A commitment that we will obey Him! Here are two verses for us to consider and meditate on…

Psalm 119:112 NASB *"I have inclined my heart to perform Your statutes. Forever, even to the end."*

Psalm 119:33 NASB *"Teach me, O LORD, the way of Your statutes, And I shall observe it to the end."*

We see in these verses and in the entire psalm, an attitude of a loving heart that desires to follow and obey God, and an attitude that is committed to following the Law of God continually. That must be our attitude as well.

James says that the law is not only perfect, but it is also the law of liberty. What is this perfect law and what is this law of liberty? It is the entire moral law of God from the Old and New Testament.

Thomas D. Lea, in his commentary on James, explains it this way: "The Law is perfect because it provides a full, complete disclosure of God through Jesus Christ. It provides freedom in that it gives liberty to those who submit to its authority. This liberty provides a victory over the bondage of habits and attitudes which can overpower human will. It also provides freedom in that the power of the Holy Spirit becomes available to strengthen believers to a new quality of spiritual life."

In other words, the perfect law of God through Christ can give us victory over sin in the power of the Holy Spirit so that we can become more like Christ.

2 Corinthians 3:17–18 NASB *"Now the Lord is the Spirit, and where the Spirit of the Lord is, there is liberty. But we all, with unveiled face, beholding as in a mirror the glory of the Lord, are being transformed into the same image from glory to glory, just as from the Lord, the Spirit."*

The law of God is liberating because it makes available to us through our Lord and Savior Jesus Christ, and the power of the Holy Spirit, the life we were created to live. No one is freer than when they are living the life, they were created to live by obeying the Word of God. We will only live in this freedom if we are quick to obey, not putting off repentance until later. If we put off repentance until later, for most of us "later" never comes; because as James says, we forget.

As we hear the word of God and it exposes to us our sin, if we do not immediately repent and purpose in our hearts to turn from our sin, the sermon ends, or our time of personal devotion is over. The cares of life enter back in, the point of conviction is gone, and we remain a forgetful hearer.

But the person who pays close attention looks intently at the perfect law of liberty, does the work of obedience, and does not forget what he has heard, this man will be blessed in what he does. The Greek word for "blessed" here is the same as when Lyndon preached through the Beatitudes in Matthew 5. The meaning here for "blessed" is "happy."

So, if we are paying close attention, looking intently at the perfect law of liberty, and if we immediately repent of our sin and do the work of consistent obedience, not forgetting what we have heard, then we will be happy in what we do. Because what we do, our actions, and our behavior, will be in line with the character and purposes of God. We will be moving forward in becoming more like Christ!

Psalm 119:2 NASB *"How blessed are those who observe His testimonies, Who seek Him with all their heart."*

James 1:23–25 NASB *"For if anyone is a hearer of the word and not a doer, he is like a man who looks at his natural face in a mirror; for once he has looked at himself and gone away, he has immediately forgotten what kind of person he was. But one who looks intently at the perfect law, the law of liberty, and abides by it, not having become a forgetful hearer but an effectual doer, this man will be blessed in what he does."*

Remember the story of Narcissus? He's the proud, beautiful man in the Greek myth who saw his reflection in a pool, fell in love with it, couldn't tear himself away, and it killed him.

All of us sinners are Narcissistic to some degree, but the enchanting power that mirrors have over most of us is different from Narcissus. When we look into a mirror, most of us are not captivated by our beauty, we are condemned by our defects.

For us, mirrors are not just things that hang on our walls. Fallen, proud hearts turn just about everything into a mirror. Magazines, mall browsing, mutual fund reports, someone else's immaculate lawn or impressive children, a beautiful home, a successful business, or a growing church can all become mirrors; because when we look at them, we see reflections of ourselves. We see ourselves wanting in comparison.

So, the enchantment ends up being a Narcissistic obsession without changing our self-image into a thing of beauty, usually into the constantly changing, illusive images of what the world tells us is beautiful. The power we desire our improved image to have is not to enchant ourselves by looking at our direct reflection, but to be enchanted by other people's admiration of us.

Other people's admiration is our pool of Narcissus.

This is why focusing on our self-image is so dangerous. Many of us do need our sin-corrupted, Satan-encouraged self-loathing corrected. But this will never happen by focusing on our self-image because our salvation, peace, and happiness are not found in improving our image or having the fleeting pleasure of others' admiration. We are not designed to be satisfied with our own glory. We are designed to be satisfied with God's glory (Romans 1:23), and however much we would like to be like God (Genesis 3:5). We never will be, not even close.

CHAPTER TWO: THE IMAGE OF GOD

Not the Soul

Genesis 1:26–27 says that God made humankind in his "image" and "likeness." Both terms mean the same thing, and so this is usually referred to as the "image of God" (*imago dei*).

Some understand the image of God to mean those qualities that make us human, for example: possessing a soul, higher-order reasoning, self-consciousness, consciousness of God, and the ability to have a relationship with him. This seems like a good definition, since only humans are in God's image, and these are qualities that make us human.

Understanding the image of God as the soul also helps some people reconcile evolution and Christianity. Somewhere along the evolutionary line, God gave two hominids immortal souls, thus becoming the first true human beings. In other words, despite the lengthy evolutionary process, humans were "created" only at this point. These two "souled" hominids are Adam and Eve. Some say this could have happened about 10,000 years ago, which would line things up nicely with the rough chronology presented in Genesis.

I understand the motivation for this explanation: to maintain somehow the biblical description of human origin in the face of evolution, but I am fairly skeptical about it. For one thing, it is a complete guesswork. It is also difficult to see what is gained here. *Preserving* the biblical description of human origins this way means it has to be *adjusted* well beyond what it says.

More importantly, equating the image of God with the soul or other qualities that make us human puts a burden on the scripture above, which brings us to the next point.

God's Representative Rulers

The image of God is important theologically, and the topic is open for discussion—but it is not a free-for-all. Genesis, other Old Testament passages, and Israel's surrounding culture give us a good idea of what the image of God means.

Many scholars draw a parallel between the image of God in Genesis and the images of kings in the ancient world. Rulers could not be everywhere at once, and travel was slow. So, they would erect monuments or statues of themselves throughout their kingdoms. These "images" let everyone know that the king's rule extended wherever his image was found.

Another kind of image in the ancient world was an idol, a physical object that represented the god in the temple. Idols were not considered gods themselves. They were statues that let you know the god was in some mysterious sense "present."

Statues of kings and gods help us understand what it means for humans to be made in God's image: humans are placed in God's kingdom as his *representatives*.

J. Richard Middleton (Roberts Wesleyan College) puts it well in *The Liberating Image*. He offers that the image of God describes "the royal office or calling of human beings as God's representatives and agents in the world." The image of God means that humans have been given the "power to share in God's rule or the administration of the earth's resources and creatures."

When one reads Genesis 1:26–27 with this in mind, the point becomes fairly obvious:

"Let us make humankind in our *image*, according to our *likeness, and let them have dominion* over the fish… birds… cattle… wild animals… creeping things" (NRSV).

Humankind, created on the sixth day, has been given the authority to rule over the other creatures God had made on the fourth and fifth days. They have that authority because humankind is made in God's image.

There is nothing here about a soul, the ability to reason, being conscious of God, or any other psychological or spiritual trait. As John Walton points out, as important as these qualities are for making us human, they do not *define* what the image of God means in Genesis. Rather, those qualities are *tools* that serve humans in their image-bearing role.

The phrase "image of God" is not about what makes us human. It is about humanity's unique role in being God's kingly representatives in creation. Once we understand what the image of God means in Genesis, we will be in a better position to see how this idea is worked out elsewhere in the Bible.

No Idols

In ancient Mesopotamia, *every* nation had pantheons of gods and they *all* worshipped their gods through images. Israel's first two Commandments were wholly out of sync with the ancient world. The Israelites were told: "I am the only God you will worship" (Exodus 20:3), and "don't worship any images whatsoever" (20:4–6). The Second Commandment includes making images of Yahweh, which the Israelites broke in the golden calf incident in Exodus 32.

There are two reasons why Israel was told not to make images of Yahweh. First, unlike the other gods, Yahweh is distinct from what he has made. He cannot be captured by a carved image of animals or any other piece of creation.

Second, God already made an image of himself: humankind, a living image. By carving images to worship Yahweh, Israel would be creating an alternate "connection" with Yahweh.

Israel's King as God's Image

There is another important angle to bring into the picture. In the ancient Mesopotamian world, kings were the representative rulers of the gods; they ruled the people on behalf of the gods. Kings were considered god-like, sometimes referred to as the "sons" of one god or another, and often worshipped as gods.

Look at Psalm 2. This psalm is about the coronation of Israel's king. This king is no ordinary man: he is *God's* "anointed one" (v. 2). God himself installed this king "on Zion, my holy hill" (v. 6).

The heart of the psalm is v. 7. God says to the king, "You are my son; today I have become your father." God has put Israel's king—his son—on the throne to rule the people on his behalf. This father-son relationship between Yahweh and the king lines up with ancient Mesopotamian thinking. It also has some implications for understanding Jesus.

Unlike the other nations, Israelite kings were never worshipped. Israel even had a skeptical attitude toward kingship (e.g., 1 Samuel 8). In fact, kings were every bit as subject to God's rule as anyone else (hence, the prophets were free to call kings to account). But they still were anointed to embody the royal image-bearing role. Israel's history of kingship is so tragic because the kings largely failed to reflect this image.

Humankind in God's Image

Unique to Israel, the role of a royal image-bearer was conferred not only on a line of kings but also on *all* people—a striking notion in the ancient world.

Psalm 8:4-6 aptly summarizes what the "image of God" means.

4—What is *man* that you are mindful of him, the *son of man* that you care for him?

5—You have made him a *little lower than God* and crowned him with *glory and honor*.

6—You have made him *ruler* over the works of your hands; you put *everything under his feet*.

A common Christian reaction when reading Psalms 8 is to say, "Surely this can't describe "man" in general. It must be talking about Jesus." Not so fast. Rather, read this psalm in light of Genesis 1:26-27.

This psalm speaks of the high status of *humanity*. Just as in English, "man" here means "humanity." The singular pronouns "him" and "his" simply reflect the fact that "man" is grammatically singular (we do the same in English). Likewise, it is tempting to read "son of man" in verse 4 and jump ahead to the New Testament and think it means Jesus. It doesn't (not here, not yet). It simply means "human."

So "man" is made "a little lower than God" (v. 5). This is striking—in fact, the NIV puts a bit of a damper on it by translating "God" as "heavenly beings." In a footnote, though, the NIV adds "God" as a possible reading. NRSV has "God." Jewish Publication Society (Tanakh) has "the divine."

We shouldn't get too hung up on that point. The Hebrew (Elohim) can mean either one, and it doesn't matter much in the end. "Heavenly beings" fits nicely with "let *us* make" in Genesis 1:26—a reference to a heavenly divine court, a common idea in the ancient world. ("Us" is not a reference to the Trinity, which would have made no sense to Israelites, as John Calvin pointed out hundreds of years ago.) Humans are one step below God and his divine council.

If Elohim means "God," that also reflects Genesis 1:26–27. Humans as the pinnacle of creation, the only beings made in God's image. Either way, the point is that being human is a big deal.

The rest of verse 5 and verse 6 fill out what "a little lower than God" means. Humans are "crowned with glory and honor" (v. 5), a phrase typically reserved for God. They also rule over the work of God's hands (v. 6), a clear allusion to Genesis 1:26–27. The psalmist even goes so far as to say that God has put everything under humanity's feet.

This psalm is a great summary of what the image of God means. There is nothing in all of creation that has a higher status than humanity. There is nothing in all of creation that is more god-like than humanity. The psalm is picked up by the author of Hebrews to speak of Jesus.

One of the portraits the New Testament paints of Jesus is that of the ultimate image-bearer of God. Jesus fully reflects God's image; he is the true representative of God in his creation. No one embodies more fully this truly human quality.

Psalm 8 praises God for how he has exalted humanity: man is a little lower than God, crowned with glory and honor, and everything has been placed under his feet. Humankind, in other words, is one step below God, given authority to rule creation. Psalm 8 is fully consistent with Genesis 1:26–27 where the "image of God" is described as ruling over all of creation.

In Hebrews 2:5–9, the anonymous author cites Psalm 8 for a reason that might not be obvious at first glance: Jesus ranks higher than angels, a topic he began in 1:5. (In fact, all of Hebrews is one long "Jesus is better than…" argument, e.g. Moses, the high priest, and the tabernacle.)

Psalm 8 supports his argument. Creation was not subject to angels, but *humankind*. The author of Hebrews reminds us that "everything" is put under human royal authority—everything is subject to humans (v. 8). But the author of Hebrews laments, "Yet at present we do not see everything subject to him" (v. 8). The "him" refers to humanity. What we do see, however, is Jesus who is *now* crowned with glory and honor because of his death (v. 9).

It is not to angels that he has subjected the world to come, about which we are speaking. But there is a place where someone has testified: "What is man that you are mindful of him, the son of man that you care for him? You made him a little[a] lower than the angels; you crowned him with glory and honor and put everything under his feet."

In putting everything under him, God left nothing that is not subject to him. Yet at present, we do not see everything subject to him. But we see Jesus, who was made a little lower than the angels, now crowned with glory and honor because he suffered death, so that by the grace of God he might taste death for everyone.

Jesus, who is like his brothers and sisters in every way (2:17), is the "ultimate human" because everything is under his authority. The lofty status of humanity as God's royal image-bearers, however true, is not fully realized in humanity as a whole. It is fully realized in Jesus as, paradoxically, the *crucified* and resurrected Son of God.

Jesus is the *true* image-bearer. You might say that Jesus is the only truly and fully human figure who has ever lived. By looking at the crucified and risen Son, we see what "human" really means, not the corrupted dysfunctional version that stares back at us from the mirror, or that we see in others.

Colossians 1:15–20 makes the same point in a different way. Jesus is the "image of the invisible God" (v. 15): he rules creation because all things were created by him. It is understandable to read this passage and think it is only focusing on Jesus' divinity, but that would be missing half the point. As the resurrected son, Jesus is "head of the body, the church, the beginning and firstborn from among the dead" (v. 18). By his resurrection, Jesus is the first to embody fully the image-bearing role conferred on all humanity in Genesis.

Jesus does this not for himself, but for those who would come after, the people of God. Jesus is not simply an "over all creation." He is "*firstborn* over all creation" (v. 15). Christians, in other words, go along for the ride. As *firstborn* over creation, he sees to it that those born after would achieve that same status. Simply put, in his resurrection, Jesus "completes" Genesis 1:26–27 for him and us.

For this reason, he had to be made like his brothers in every way, so that he might become a merciful and faithful high priest in service to God, and that he might make atonement for the sins of the people.

This theme is already announced at the beginning of Hebrews 1:1–4. In the past, God had spoken through prophets, but now he is speaking through the Son he has appointed. The echo of Psalm 2 where Israel's king is God's appointed Son, is confirmed in v. 5 where the author cites

Psalm 2:7. As Son, Jesus is the newly appointed Davidic king, the representative ruler. But this Son takes it up a notch: he is the "radiance of God's glory and the *exact representation* of his being." Jesus is God's representative ruler like no other.

The image of God in Genesis is not about "what makes us human," such as one's soul. It is about the lofty role God has given humankind to be his representative ruler. That is what "image means": nothing more — but nothing less.

He is the image of the invisible God, the firstborn of all creation. For by him, all things were created: things in heaven and on earth, visible and invisible, whether thrones or powers or rulers or authorities; all things were created by him and for him. He is before all things, and in him, all things hold together. He is the head of the body, the church; he is the beginning and the firstborn from among the dead, so that in everything he might have the supremacy. For God was pleased to have all his fullness dwell in him, and through him to reconcile to himself all things, whether things on earth or things in heaven, by making peace through his blood, shed on the cross.

Understood this way, we can and should speak of the image of God as marred, incomplete, and subject to sin in all of us. The true image of God is only realized in the crucified and risen Son of God. This gives us a much fuller understanding of the incarnation. The incarnate Son of God is fully God and *fully human*.

Jesus is the full image-bearer of God. He is the most human of any human who has ever lived. By faith, we too participate in restored humanity.

Jesus is the complete human and true image-bearer of God. He is the exact representation of God, the ruler over creation. That "completed humanity" is conferred upon those who believe that Jesus is Christ. The image is marred in humanity in general; it is restored in the man, Jesus. All those who are "in Christ" (as Paul likes to put it) participate in the restored humanity that began at Jesus' resurrection. The new humanity is open to all, but the entryway is through the risen Messiah.

So, what does it mean for Christians to be image-bearers of God? It means we are called to live daily in such a way that *embodies more* what that image looks like. Jesus is both the *cause* of our renewed image and the *model* we follow as we try to live that way.

This brings us to a paradox that is central to how Christians see themselves as re-created in God's image. Jesus elevated humanity to its true image-bearing role, but his incarnation was an act of emptying himself of his divine right, as Paul says in Philippians 2:6–7. Jesus humbled himself (v. 8). Incarnation is an act of humiliation.

For Christians, too, participating in the renewed image of God means following Christ in both his exaltation and humiliation. Simply put, we bear the renewed image of God daily as our lives conform to Jesus.'

Paul sums up the matter nicely in Philippians 3:10. Knowing Christ—which is never a simple mental activity but a life path—means experiencing both the power of his resurrection and the fellowship of sharing in his suffering. Those who are part of this new humanity in Christ bear the marks of Jesus' exaltation and humiliation every day.

Being part of the renewed image of God means being "conformed to the image" of Jesus (Romans 8:29). We become increasingly like him in *every* way.

Christians are now full representatives of God in his creation, but not in the ancient Near Eastern sense — or even Old Testament sense — of a ruler. I am not dismissing that, but "rule" is not the New Testament's emphasis. The emphasis has now moved to other things. Christians represent God to all of creation through humility, love, and holiness.

One of the many passages that reminds us of this is I Peter 2:9–12. Borrowing language from the Exodus, Peter tells his readers that they are a "chosen people, a royal priesthood, a holy nation, and a people belonging to God" (v. 9). This lofty status does not just make them part of the "God club." They are God's people who live such good lives among the inhabitants of the world "that they may see [their] good deeds and glorify God on the day he visits us" (v. 12).

You may have heard the expression "Be careful how you act. You may be the only Bible people ever read." That's a good point, but the reality is much more severe. We represent to the world what God has done in Christ, so a better phrase might be, "Be careful how you act. You may be the only Jesus people ever see."

This is beyond what Genesis 1:26–27 was about in its original context. There is nothing there about humility, suffering with Christ, or living godly lives. This is true. But what Jesus does to the image of God in Genesis 1:26–27 is what he does with everything else in the Old Testament: he *transforms* it and fills it out beyond its limited Old Testament meaning that the shadow gives way to reality.

Still, there is one more dimension of the renewed image of God that looks more like what we see in the Old Testament. It is not a dominant theme, but it is there, nonetheless. In 2 Timothy 2:13, we read that enduring present suffering has a not yet realized future dimension: "If we endure, we will also reign with him."

I don't know what this means, but it seems that the final step of the Christian journey is some type of eschatological ruling authority. This is not explained anywhere—and I am not going to venture a guess as to what this looks like. Suffice it to say that there is "something more" to what Christ in his resurrection has already done in restoring the image of God. The New Testament is more concerned with how God's people here embody Jesus' life of servant-leadership.

God made humanity in his image. This image has a focused meaning in the Old Testament— being God's representative ruler over his creation. That image was marred and eventually restored and transformed in Jesus, the Son of

Man, and the exact representation of the image of God. Those who are in Christ take part in this new humanity.

CHAPTER THREE: WE ARE DESIGNED TO BE SATISFIED WITH GOD'S GLORY

The gospel we need won't be viewed in our mirrors. For that, we need to look through a window and that's what the Bible is. The Bible is not a mirror; it is a window. It is through the Bible that we come to see reality. It is through the Bible that we see the:

2 Corinthians 4:4 NKJV *"…Gospel of the glory of Christ who is the image of God."*

John 1:29 ESV *"Behold, the Lamb of God, who takes away the sin of the world."*

Psalm 17:15 *"As for me, I will behold thy face in righteousness: I shall be satisfied, when I awake, with thy likeness."*

The health and restoration of your sin-sick, Narcissistic soul, lies in looking to Jesus (Hebrews 12:2). It is not a better *you* that you need to see. You need to see Jesus and then bask in the amazing truth that the more you look to him and trust him, the more you will be conformed to his beautiful image (Romans 8:29). Also, by being in Christ, you have received and will receive as a gift (Romans 6:23) all that will make you most satisfied and most truly beautiful (Ephesians 1:3).

Narcissus is a pagan parable of a real danger. Beware of mirrors—any kind of mirror. Look at mirrors as little as possible. Instead, look through a window. Any window is ten times healthier for you than a mirror. But especially look through the window of God's word so you can see Jesus.

He is the Savior (1 John 4:14), the peace (Ephesians 2:14), and the satisfying gain (Philippians 3:8) you are looking for.

John Piper, said, "I believe all of you somewhere within your heart want to be the instruments of God's power, and therefore, even if you don't feel like it now, there is buried somewhere in your subconscious the longing to be a man or a woman of fervent and effective prayer."

He explains how he knows this: The reason I am confident of this is that every one of you is created in God's image. Each one of you was created to be a conscious mirror of God's image. You were created to consciously reflect his glory like a mirror of God's image. Before sin entered the world, I think Adam and Eve had an overwhelming longing to be used by God to image-forth his power, wisdom, and love in the world. They wanted to be mirrors of his glory.

That longing is deep within every person today, but it has been distorted by sin. In a sense, the distortion is only slight; but it is the difference between day and night. It is the difference between wanting to reflect his face and wanting to take his place.

Piper explains the glory and function of a mirror, starting in the Garden:

The glory of a mirror is to put its face to the light and to let that light shine. This is what mirrors are made for. This is the deep longing of the heart, but sin entered the world, and its first manifestation was Adam and Eve's discontent with being mirrors. They began to want to be their own source of light. They began to feel that mirrors were just glass with a thin black coating of tin and mercury.

They suddenly became conscious of the fact that to be a good mirror, you have to turn whichever way the light moves. You can't be your own master. So, they chose to be their source of light; they turned their brilliant mirror faces away from God, and now all they can do is block his light and cast a shadow across the world.

I want you to see that the longing of Adam and Eve to *be* the light is a distortion of a legitimate longing, namely, to *reflect* the light. The Bible teaches that everyone since the fall of Adam and Eve is born with these same distorted longings. We come into the world longing to be God. We want the world to revolve around our interests.

We want to decide for ourselves which way to turn our faces. We want people to esteem us, admire us, and compliment us. We don't like the thought of being a mirror that has no beauty except in the thing it reflects. We don't like the idea of having to turn our face wherever the light wants to go. We want to be our light. We want to be God.

This comes with our fallen humanity. It is the very essence of sin. If you are honest, you will admit that you have felt this way; but this universal experience of sin is Satan's distortion of something wonderful. The wonderful thing is the pure and righteous longing to be used by God to reflect his glory in the world.

It's not wrong to want to be significant. It's wrong to want your significance to reside in yourself instead of in the one you reflect. It's not wrong to want to be important. It's wrong to want your importance to be in yourself instead of the one you reflect. It's not wrong to boast, but "Let him who boasts, boast in the Lord!"

Concealed deep beneath our pride, our craving for esteem, and our love of power and influence is a good thing that has been distorted, namely, the longing to be a mirror of God. To be a mirror of God is the highest honor to which a creature can aspire. The most ludicrous sight in the world is a created mirror turning away from the light of God and then trying on its own to make a little spark to brighten the shadow it casts on the world.

Piper goes on to apply this to prayer, which is a way we mirror God:

A mirror faces away from itself to its source of light so that it might have some use in the world, and prayer faces away from itself toward God so that it might be of some use in the world.

A mirror is designed to receive light and channel it for the good of others, and prayer is designed to receive grace and channel it for the good of others.

The value of a mirror is not in itself but in its potential to let something else be seen. The value of prayer is not in itself but in its potential to let the power and beauty of God be seen.

A mirror is utterly dependent on the source of light from outside itself, and prayer is the posture of the childlike, utterly dependent on the resources and kindness of the heavenly Father.

So, praying is the way we mirror God. If I am right that each of you, in the image of God, has a deep desire to be a mirror of God, then it is also true that, even if you don't feel like it now, there is buried somewhere in your subconscious the longing to be a man or a woman of fervent and effective prayer.

Beholding the Word of God is like looking in a mirror. We see two things: We understand what God is like, and unfortunately, we also find out more about ourselves and our desires. God did not give us His Word for our affirmation and reinforcement. Instead, Scripture should motivate us to change, and one of the changes it tells us we need to make is to deny ourselves, take up our cross, and follow Him (Matt 16:24; Mark 8:34; Luke 9:23).

Some of us look into the mirror of God's Word, and don't want to see who we are — we want to forget our sins, push them aside, and ignore it all. Sometimes we distort the meaning of His Word so that it fits into our lives.

James tells us, *"Anyone who listens to the word but does not do what it says is like someone who looks at his face in a mirror and, after looking at himself, goes away and immediately forgets what he looks like. But whoever looks intently into the perfect law that gives freedom, and continues in it — not forgetting what they have heard, but doing it — they will be blessed in what they do"* James 1:23–25 NIV.

"The Word of the Lord is a revealer of secrets; it shows a man his life, his thoughts, his heart, his inmost self."

– Charles Spurgeon

Christ's directive to renunciate ourselves is reported three times in Scripture and each writer gives us a slightly different set of details surrounding its utterance.

Matthew, writing to the Jews, tells us Jesus spoke to His disciples. Matthew says, "You disciples are going to have to say no to yourselves, take up your cross, and follow Jesus because that's a characteristic of a disciple."

Mark includes another group. "He summoned the crowd with His disciples, and said to them, 'If anyone wishes to come after Me, he must deny himself, and take up his cross and follow Me,'" (Mark 8:34 NASB). As he records Jesus's words, not only for the disciples but for the multitudes as well, he wants readers to know what it means to be a disciple.

Luke puts it all together for a general audience. He writes, "Then he said to them all: 'Whoever wants to be my disciple must deny themselves and take up their cross daily and follow me'" (9:23, emphasis added). Note the addition to "take up their cross daily." Later, Luke adds, "And whoever does not carry their cross and follow me cannot be my disciple" (14:27).

Why would God ask a Christian to deny himself or herself? The answer is in Galatians 5:16–17 which says, *"So I say, walk by the Spirit, and you will not gratify the desires of the flesh. For the flesh desires what is contrary to the Spirit, and the Spirit what is contrary to the flesh. They are in conflict with each other, so that you are not to do whatever you want."*

Remember Luke writes to tell us we're to forsake what we want to do to follow Christ—to focus our lives on Him, every day, in everything we do.

So, how do we escape from wanting to do our own thing? The only way we can deny ourselves is with the help of the most powerful One in the universe. He is the One who offers us the way from sin and self. He provides the bridge from living for ourselves to following Christ.

That bridge is the cross—how a person comes into a relationship with Christ, and how the committed disciple finds freedom from sins and self in the ongoing challenges of the Christian life.

CHAPTER FOUR: MIRRORING YOURSELF THROUGH THE WORD OF GOD

When the light of God shines on our pathway, we can navigate our way through life. But it is of no use to just navigate our pathways through life, without allowing the light of God to illuminate our inner man, so that we can be able to see through ourselves. This is what the word of God also does for us.

James 1:22–25 NIV *"Do not merely listen to the word, and so deceive yourselves. Do what it says. Anyone who listens to the word but does not do what it says is like someone who looks at his face in a mirror and, after looking at himself, goes away and immediately forgets what he looks like. But whoever looks intently into the perfect law that gives freedom, and continues in it – not forgetting what they have heard, but doing it – they will be blessed in what they do."*

God's word is the mirror of His love in our lives. The word of God serves as the mirror of His love towards us, in showing us that no earthly work in man's wisdom, philosophy, or intellectualism, can even match up with who we are as the children of God.

You see a mirror helps us only if we can act, to correct the error in the image that is being reflected on it. If for example, we do see dirt on our facial reflection in a mirror, we are smart enough to get rid of the dirt from our face.

No lady likes to go to sleep at night with a dirty face or a made-up face. No, most ladies are smart enough to give themselves a face wash, before sleeping at the end of each day. The same thing goes with our spiritual lives, as the word of God probes through our inner man. If we observe anything in our lives, which may prevent the flow of God's love through us; we need to be smart in doing the right thing to get rid of it.

No child of God should be shy or ashamed of standing before his or her heavenly Father. We have boldness before God because we are taking the right steps, in getting rid of the spiritual dirt out of our lives. We're getting rid of the dirt which is being reflected from the mirror of God's word, as we are meditating on it.

Revelation 21: 27 NIV *"Nothing impure will ever enter it, nor will anyone who does what is shameful or deceitful, but only those whose names are written in the Lamb's book of life."*

There is no deceit or silly games with sin in the presence of God. Nothing impure or with sin in it can stand or go unnoticed in His presence. No, we are not ashamed either of who we are as the children of God. That's why we can approach Him boldly and without reproach. The mirror of the word of God can only help us to readjust in doing the right things, if only we are ready to change. If after we have opened our spiritual eyes of understanding, to see the uncleanliness in our lives; we are taking the necessary steps, to bring our lives in line with God's requirements. This is what we have to do for the love of God, to continually shine through our lives. Because we love God, we will always be prompted to do the right things. God's love will always compel us to do the right things. God's love will always make its appeal to us through His word.

Our initial response to the reflection of an unclean image on our inner man, from the mirror of God's word should always be, to receive it first as a fact of life. It is a fact, but not the truth about who we are.

The truth is about who God says that we are. There is a difference between facts and the truth. The truth has to do with God's word to us and about who we are as His children. If we can't accept the fact that is presented before us in the mirror of God's word, the reality of us being rooted and grounded in the truth, about our real identity with God will become vague.

Many have ignored the facts of their lives that they do see regularly through their meditations in God's word. They are continually living with those facts of their lives, without doing anything about them to get rid of them. They are going through life while struggling to accept the truth about who they are in God's word. They are finding it difficult to accept their real identity in Christ Jesus. This explains why they are not growing spiritually because they can't accept the facts in their lives and receive the truth about their identity in Christ Jesus.

There are so many who are relating to the dirt in their spiritual lives in this manner. The blockage of sin in their lives is preventing the flow of God's love through them. They want to love as Christ taught us to love, but they are carrying too much spiritual baggage from their pasts in their lives.

We must learn to accept whatever God has declared about us in His word, without struggling to accept it as the truth. That's how our faith works to manifest what is believed with the heart. We must learn to allow our faith to appropriate God's provision for us. The more we look into the mirror of God's word, the more we shall behold the glory that is being reflected in it (2 Corinthians 3:18), and then the lesser we will be able to see the spiritual dirt in our lives, without ignoring any one of them at all. But we would rather be doing something to get rid of them. This is how more of God's glory will be reflected through us. God's love is manifested with His glory in our lives in this way.

The Holy Spirit will transform us as long as we continue to look at the mirror of God's word. As soon as we take our spiritual eyes away from the mirror of God's word, to turn into the wisdom, theories or theologies of men, the Holy Spirit will no longer work in us, to make us perfect in love. We need to remember that it is our love walk that makes us perfect as Christians and our perfection is only in Christ Jesus.

Renew Your Mind to be Mature in Love

By meditating on the word of God, we can receive His light for direction in life. This was the blueprint for success that Joshua received from the Lord before leading the Israelites into battles.

Joshua 1:8 AMP *"This Book of the Law shall not depart from your mouth, but you shall read [and meditate on] it day and night, so that you may be careful to do [everything] in accordance with all that is written in it; for then you will make your way prosperous, and then you will be successful."*

We can discern the good from the evil of this world, as we give God's word top priority in our lives. God's word separates the thoughts of our mind, from that of our spirit man through the process of meditation. By meditating on the word of God, we can properly process the thoughts of our mind, to be able to discern what is pleasing and acceptable before God in it. This process helps us in identifying and separating those thoughts, from the thoughts of our born-again spirit man.

The mind often relies on natural knowledge to function in formulating its opinions. The opinions from our mind are often deceptive, but through the process of meditation on the promises of God, the natural knowledge is replaced by the supernatural knowledge and wisdom of God. The process of replacing our natural thoughts for the supernatural thoughts is what Paul called the — "renewing of your mind" (Romans 12:2).

Our quest and love for God's word is what triggers this in our hearts. We must understand that supernatural things never come without our effort as we approach God by faith (Hebrews 11:6). It is at the moment when our faith is active before God, that God manifests Himself to us. The renewing of the mind happens as we stop focusing on seeing the natural or physical proofs of His presence around us. In other words, when we are diligent in seeking Him through the scriptures, we will find Him — God.

The word of God that transforms us comes through the scriptures and the spoken word of the Holy Spirit into our hearts. His revealed Word then becomes sweet in our mouth, as we daily confess what we are meditating on. It brings the sweetness of God and His love into our lives; a sweetness like honey that makes His fragrance of love flow through us, in saving this world of reckless and restless sinners.

His love has been shed on our hearts by the Holy Spirit. That is why the works of our hands as Christians will always be fruitful and successful. Real success in life comes as we meditate on His word day and night.

Are you confused about a decision that you need to take on an issue right now? Turn to the word of God for the green light and direction to get you to where you need to be in life. Stop trying to figure things out in your own way or through earthly wisdom. God's word gives His wisdom to a heart that is open and discerning to hear from Him. Let the love of God move you to start transforming your life with the power of His word today. God is not finished with you yet. You are God's perfect work in progress. You are loved by God.

Mirroring God through Prayers

Concealed deep beneath our pride and our craving for esteem and our love of power and influence is a good thing that has been distorted, namely, the longing to be a mirror of God. To be a mirror of God is the highest honor to which a creature can aspire.

The most ludicrous sight in the world is a created mirror turning away from the light of God and then trying on its own to make a little spark to brighten the shadow it casts on the world.

Now, how can you mirror God through prayer? What I have been trying to show is that each of you, if not consciously, at least subconsciously wants to be a person of fervent and powerful prayer. That is, you want to have a significant place in the purposes of God. You want to be his instrument in accomplishing something worthwhile.

My argument for this has been that behind the universal desire to be God, there is a distorted longing to be a mirror of God - to have the significance and the importance of reflecting the glory of God. But my unspoken assumption so far is that *praying is the way we mirror God.*

Surely that is easy to see. A mirror faces away from itself to its source of light so that it might have some use in the world, and prayer faces away from itself toward God so that it might be of some use in the world. A mirror is designed to receive light and channel it for the good of others, and prayer is designed to receive grace and channel it for the good of others.

The value of a mirror is not in itself, but in its potential to let something else be seen. The value of prayer is not in itself, but in its potential to let the power and beauty of God be seen. A mirror is utterly dependent on the source of light from outside itself, and prayer is the posture of the childlike, utterly dependent on the resources and kindness of the heavenly Father.

Praying is the way we mirror God. If each of you, in the image of God, has a deep desire to be a mirror of God, then it is also true that, even if you don't feel like it now, there is buried somewhere in your subconscious, the longing to be a man or a woman of fervent and effective prayer.

My prayer is that God will use this message to bring that desire to the surface and make it insatiable to all.

God's Word Triumphs through Prayer

One of the texts that has done that for my desire to pray is 2 Thessalonians 3:1–2. It's short, but full of incentives for those of us who want to have a significant role in God's purposes:

"Finally, brethren, pray for us, that the word of the Lord may have free course, and be glorified, even as it is with you, and that we may be delivered from unreasonable and wicked men; for all men have not faith."

This text gives tremendous significance to prayer for God's victorious purposes. We could state the doctrine like this: Through prayer, the word of the Lord overcomes obstacles and reaches a glorious victory.

CHAPTER FIVE: THE VEIL IN OUR LIVES

2 Corinthians 3:18 NKJV *"But we all with unveiled face, beholding as in a mirror the glory of the Lord, are being transformed into the same image from glory to glory, just as by the Spirit of the Lord."*

Here, the apostle Paul likened us believers to a mirror. A mirror is a surface that both beholds and reflects what's in front of it. But if the mirror is covered, or veiled, it can't behold or reflect anything. It has to be unveiled.

In the same way, if we believers are to behold the glory of the Lord—that is, to see Him and gaze upon His beautiful and glorious Person—we must have an unveiled face. So, what does it mean to have an unveiled face?

What is a Veil?

To see what it means to have an unveiled face, we first have to see what a veil is. For this, let's read:

2 Corinthians 3:15 NKJV *"But even to this day, when Moses is read, a veil lies on their heart."*

Here, the apostle Paul was speaking of the Jewish people, who revered the writings of Moses in the Old Testament. It wasn't the writings of Moses themselves, but what the Jewish people thought they knew about them that became a veil on their hearts. Because of this, they couldn't see that the writings of Moses revealed the Lord Jesus.

We know this from the Lord's word in Luke 24. This chapter gives the account of the resurrected Jesus meeting and conversing with two of His disciples on the road to Emmaus. Verse 27 says:

"And beginning from Moses and from all the prophets, He explained to them clearly in all the Scriptures the things concerning Himself."

Jesus made it clear that the writings of Moses and even the entire Old Testament were concerning Himself. These writings revealed not a religion for people to follow but a wonderful Person, Jesus Christ.

Yet the Jewish people couldn't see this because Paul said that they had a veil on their hearts. Many verses in the Bible reveal that our heart is composed of our mind, emotion, will, and our conscience. Our heart is the organ with which we love God, people, and things. Our heart is also the gateway of our being, determining whether we're open or closed to particular people and matters.

Our heart is central to our relationship with God, so the condition of our heart is crucial. If we have a veil on our hearts, how can we see God? How can He infuse Himself into us? To have a veiled heart is a serious matter.

What Veils Do We Have?

What about us today? We may think that we know who Jesus is, so Paul's word in 2 Corinthians 3 doesn't apply to us.

But we need to realize that in principle, a veil can lie on our hearts at any time. Sinful things are certainly a problem between us and God, and we need to take care of those things. From the example Paul used of the Jewish people, we can see that even things related to God and His Word can be a problem for us. Anything that arises from preconceived notions or assumptions about the Word is a veil that covers our hearts and prevents us from beholding the Lord.

For instance, we may have certain ideas about how we should worship God, how to please God, or how to live the Christian life. These ideas can preoccupy us and prevent us from seeing the Lord.

Not only so, things that seem harmless or unrelated to our Christian walk, such as our personal philosophy or cultural traditions, can also become a veil that covers our hearts.

Since this is the case, what can we do? How can we have the veils removed from our hearts?

Turning Our Hearts to the Lord

The answer to this question is twofold and involves both our heart and our spirit, our deepest part.

In relation to our heart, 2 Corinthians 3:16 NASB says:

"But whenever a heart turns to the Lord, the veil is taken away."

What an encouraging word! Note 1 on this verse in the Recovery Version tells us:

"This indicates that when their heart is away from the Lord, the veil lies on their heart. When their heart turns to the Lord, the veil is taken away. Actually, their turned-away heart is the veil. To turn their heart to the Lord is to take away the veil."

So, we need to ask ourselves, is our heart turned away from the Lord or turned to the Lord?

Whenever we sense that we can't see the Lord, we must turn away from whatever is occupying us and turn our hearts to the Lord. We don't want to hold onto or treasure any of our concepts or views; we simply want Him, and we want to see Him as He is.

To turn our hearts to the Lord, we can pray something like this:

"Lord Jesus, I love You. I don't want to hold onto any of my thoughts or assumptions about You. I just want You. I want to behold You, Lord. So, I turn my heart to You right now."

The Word of God assures us that whenever we turn our heart to the Lord, the veil is taken away.

Exercising Our Spirit

Next, in relation to our spirit, 2 Corinthians 3:17 NKJV says:

"Now the Lord is the Spirit; and where the Spirit of the Lord is, there is liberty."

For us to experience the freedom mentioned here, we must realize who Christ is today and where He is. This verse tells us that the resurrected Lord, Christ, is the Spirit.

And where is the Spirit of the Lord? 2 Timothy 4:22 KJV says:

"The Lord Jesus Christ be with thy spirit."

The day we believed in Him, the Lord as the Spirit came into our spirit and now dwells there.

Since the Lord is in our spirit, we must exercise, or use, our spirit to contact Him. This is how we can experience freedom from everything that preoccupies us.

We can exercise our spirit by praying to Him, reading His Word, and calling upon His name.

Beholding and Reflecting the Lord

When our heart is turned to Him and our spirit is exercised, we experience what is written in 2 Corinthians 3:18:

"But we all with unveiled face, with unveiled face, beholding as in a mirror the glory of the Lord, are being transformed into the same image from glory to glory, just as by the Spirit of the Lord."

Note 3 on the *unveiled face* in the Recovery Version says:

"In contrast to the veiled mind, the veiled heart (vv. 14–15). That our face is unveiled means that our heart has turned to the Lord, so that the veil has been taken away, and the Lord as the Spirit has freed us from the bondage, the veiling, of the law, so that there is no more insulation between us and the Lord."

How good it is to be unveiled! When we have no veil on our hearts and no insulation between us and the Lord, we can behold the Lord.

This verse also speaks of reflecting. Note 4 explains:

"To behold the glory of the Lord is to see the Lord ourselves; to reflect the glory of the Lord is to enable others to see Him through us."

The Result of Beholding the Lord

As we behold the Lord, something marvelous happens within us. Note 7 on *being transformed* in 2 Corinthians 3:18 explains:

"When we with unveiled face are beholding and reflecting the glory of the Lord, He infuses us with the elements of what He is and what He has done. Thus, we are being transformed metabolically to have our lives shaped by His life power with His life essence; that is, we are being transfigured, mainly by the renewing of our mind (Rom. 12:2), into His image. *Being transformed* indicates that we are in the process of transformation."

By the Lord infusing us with the elements of what He is and what He's done, a spiritual metabolic process takes place within us: we're being transformed into the same glorious image of the Lord. As a result of this ongoing process, we will express God, and God's plan for us will be fulfilled.

As we take the time to gaze upon the Lord and behold Him, His thoughts, feelings, and intentions will gradually become ours, and we'll reflect Christ to the people around us. Let's all practice turning our hearts to the Lord, spending time in fellowship with Him, and exercising our spirits every day so we can experience this wonderful, life-long process.

Now, how does a believer behold the mirror of the glory of the Lord in 2 Corinthians 3:18?

Adam was created as a perfect human being and reflected God's glory, however, he sinned, and as his descendants, we have all inherited sin, and so fall short of the glory of God. Paul declares: "*For all have sinned and fall short of the glory of God* (Rom. 3:23 NASB).

Christians are admonished to do all things for the glory of God: "*Whether, then, you eat or drink or whatever you do, do all to the glory of God*" (1 Corinthians 10:31 NASB). However, to glorify God, we have to get to know Him first.

John wrote: "*This is eternal life, that they may know You, the only true God, and Jesus Christ whom You have sent.*" (John 17:3 NASB).

Admittedly, it is not an easy task as Psalm 51:5 NLT says, "*For I was born a sinner, yes, from the moment my mother conceived me.*"

However, God will measure how well we strive to get to know him and to achieve his standards so that we can reflect his glory. We can do this by meditating on the scriptures and by prayer.

Meditating on the Scriptures

We have to make an in-depth effort to study the scriptures and get to know our creator and his qualities so that we can improve our faith and our determination to continue restraining our sinful tendencies. Then, we can reflect the glory of God. The Psalmist wrote:

Psalm 119:11 NASB "*Your word I have treasured in my heart, That I may not sin against You.*"

By Prayer

We read in the scriptures that Jesus prayed to his Father on many occasions, to help him avoid temptation to sin. To reflect God's glory, we must also persevere in prayer, to help us serve him in a manner acceptable to him, and to protect us to resist temptation (Mat. 6:13). Paul wrote:

Romans 12:12 MEV *"Rejoice in hope, be patient in suffering, persevere in prayer."*

CHAPTER SIX: HOW TO REFLECT GOD'S GLORY

Christ Is Our Example

Jesus was born as a perfect human being, (John 1:14) and is the only one who reflected God's glory throughout his life. Although we are not perfect, Peter wrote that we should all try to follow his example:

1 Peter 2:21 NASB *"For you have been called for this purpose, since Christ also suffered for you, leaving you an example for you to follow in His steps."*

Jesus had tender warmth and feeling for others, (Mark 10:13–16). Jesus felt sympathy for the leper, and "Jesus stretched out His hand and touched him, saying, "I am willing; be cleansed" (Matthew 8:1–4). Jesus cares for others and feeds 3000 (John 6:1–13). Jesus was forgiving (Luke 5:17–26 NASB)

20 "When He saw their faith, He said to him, "Man, your sins are forgiven you."25 Immediately he rose before them, and took up that on which he lay, and departed to his own house, glorifying God."

Christians with their conduct and speech can influence others to give glory to God:

Matthew 5:16 NASB *"Let your light shine before men in such a way that they may see your good works, and glorify your Father who is in heaven."* (Compare 1 Peter 2:12)

If Christians continuously respond to God's word and become doers and not just hearers (James 1:22-25), they will be transformed from glory to glory and will reflect the glory of God:

2 Corinthians 3:18 NASB *"But we all, with unveiled face, beholding as in a mirror the glory of the Lord, are being transformed into the same image from glory to glory, just as from the Lord, the Spirit."*

Become Imitators of God

To reflect God's glory, we have to become imitators of God.

Ephesians 5:1 NASB *"Therefore be imitators of God, as beloved children."*

Since the whole world is under the influence of Satan the Devil, (1 John 5:19), Christians have to make an effort to live in a way that will not bring dishonor to God.

If you love the Lord, hate evil.

Psalm 97:10 MEV *"You who love the Lord, hate evil! He preserves the lives of His devoted ones; He delivers them from the hand of the wicked."*

Be Aware of False Prophets, Apostates and Antichrists

Jesus advised his followers to be on the watch for false prophets.

Matthew 7:15 NASB *"Beware of the false prophets, who come to you in sheep's clothing, but inwardly are ravenous wolves."*

2 Thessalonians 2:3 NASB *"Let no one in any way deceive you, for it will not come unless the apostasy comes first, and the man of lawlessness is revealed, the son of destruction."*

It is obvious that from the first century false prophets, apostates, and Antichrists have shrouded the word of God and spread deception about the teachings of Christ. Today there are thousands of Christian religions, due to the diversity of the teachings and interpretations of the scriptures, so only by reading the scriptures can you determine the Antichrist and their deceptions.

1 John 2:15 NASB *"Do not love the world nor the things in the world. If anyone loves the world, the love of the Father is not in him."*

There are many things that God hates: Satanic gore, lies, violence, pornography, horoscopes (Romans 1:24–25), and many other things to be found in the scriptures. Some others are mentioned by Paul below.

1 Corinthians 5:11 NASB *"But actually, I wrote to you not to associate with any so-called brother if he is an immoral person, or covetous, or an idolater, or a reviler, or a drunkard, or a swindler – not even to eat with such a one."*

Those who hate what is bad will not seek ways to indulge in it. On the other hand, people who do not hate it may physically refrain from it while mentally wishing that they could share in bad things.

Do Not Be Idle Gossipers and Busybodies

1 Timothy 5:13 MEV *"Besides that, they learn to be idle, and not only idle, wandering around from house to house, but also gossips and busybodies, saying what they ought not."*

God is Love

God is love and if we are to glorify God, we should be loving towards others, our family, relatives, mates, and the world in general. Cultivating love will also prevent us from sinful tendencies.

1 John 4:16–19 MEV "*And we have come to know and to believe the love that God has for us. God is love. Whoever lives in love lives in God, and God in him. In this way God's love is perfected in us, so that we may have boldness on the Day of Judgment, because as He is, so are we in this world. There is no fear in love, but perfect love casts out fear, because fear has to do with punishment. Whoever fears is not perfect in love. We love Him because He first loved us.*

A Christian's conduct and speech reflect on his faith. When observers make that connection, they see that the Christian's fine conduct is a direct result of his faith and so it brings glory to God. Jesus said:

Matthew 5:16 MEV "*Let your light so shine before men that they may see your good works and glorify your Father who is in heaven.*"

CHAPTER SEVEN: THE LIGHT OF THE WORLD

Matthew 5:14 *"Ye are the light of the world."*

We, believers, are to be the "light" that shines in the world and dispels the darkness. However, like most of the things that are stated in the Bible, we understand them much better if we understand them in the context of the whole scope of Scripture. Believers are lights, but it helps us keep that in proper perspective when we realize that our light is derivative—we get it from God. We do not originate the light, we reflect the light.

Jesus, too, recognized that he was "the light" or "a light" because he reflected the light of God. We commonly hear that Jesus said "I am the light of the world," but good translations of the New Testament show us that of the three times that Jesus referred to himself as light, only once did he say that he was "the" light, the other two times he referred to himself as "a" light.

John 9:5 YLT *"When I am in the world, I am a light of the world."*

John 12:46 YLT *"I a light to the world have come, that everyone who is believing in me–in the darkness may not remain."*

In the two verses above, Jesus referred to himself as "a" light. He knew that other people who reflected the light of God into the world were also lights. There is one time in Scripture when Jesus referred to himself as "the" light, and when we read what he said in its context, we understand why he did that.

John 8:12 NIV *"When Jesus spoke again to the people, he said, "I am the light of the world."*

Jesus made this statement while speaking at the Feast of Tabernacles (also sometimes called "the Feast of Booths," John 7:2), which is one of the three feasts that the Law of Moses said the Jews were to attend each year.

The Feast of Passover occurred in the spring, the Feast of Pentecost occurred in the summer, and the Feast of Tabernacles occurred in the fall, usually our September. The way it was celebrated at the Time of Christ, the Feast of Tabernacles was an eight-day feast, and the Feast of Tabernacles recorded in John 7 and 8 was the last of the three major feasts that Jesus attended before he was killed at the Passover Feast the next year.

When we read the record in John chapters 7 and 8, we can see that Jesus was trying to reveal to people that he was the Messiah but was doing so in a way that those with an open heart would understand, while those with cold hearts would not. Jesus' words and actions did indeed convince people because day after day as the Feast progressed, more and more people believed in him.

John 7:31 *"And many of the people believed on him."*

John 7:41 *"Others said, This is the Christ."*

Then, on the last day of the feast, John 8:30 says, *"As he spake these words, many believed on him."*

Thus, in the context of revealing that he was the Messiah, it makes sense that he would say he was "the" light of the world. He was not being exclusive and claiming to be the only light, he was claiming to be the major light, the promised Messiah.

The fact that Jesus said to the people, "You are the light of the world," (Matt. 5:14) shows us that he did not think of himself as the only light. We all have the privilege and responsibility to reflect God's light.

In contrast to people and even the Messiah, who all reflect the light of God, God Himself is not "a" light or even "the" light; God is "light" (1 John 1:5). In God is no darkness at all. He shines brilliantly and has done so forever. Isaiah said God would be people's everlasting light.

Isaiah 60:19 NIV *"The sun will no more be your light by day, nor will the brightness of the moon shine on you, for the LORD will be your everlasting light, and your God will be your glory."*

There is a day coming in the future when the city of God will descend from heaven (Rev. 21:2), and every saved person will be in it with God forever. In a way, we just cannot understand at this time, but the Bible foretells, that the city will be illuminated directly by the light of God, apart from the light sources we are used to today such as the sun and moon. At that time, darkness of every kind will cease to exist, and there will be no such thing as "night."

Revelation 22:5 NIV *"There will be no more night. They will not need the light of a lamp or the light of the sun, for the Lord God will give them light. And they will reign for ever and ever."*

In contrast to the future, today the light that constantly radiates from God is reflected by believers and seen by others, which is why Jesus said, "You are the light of the world."

2 Corinthians 3:18 speaks of us reflecting the light of God which we see in the person of Jesus Christ. Before we go into that, however, it is important to discuss the verse itself and see what it is saying. Reading the two versions below shows that there is disagreement among the scholars as to whether we are "beholding as in a mirror" (i.e., "looking at as in a mirror") the glory of the Lord (NASB) or are "reflecting" the glory of the Lord (NIV).

2 Corinthians 3:18 NASB *"But we all, with unveiled face, beholding as in a mirror the glory of the Lord, are being transformed into the same image from glory to glory, just as from the Lord, the Spirit."*

2 Corinthians 3:18 NIV *"And we, who with unveiled faces all reflect the Lord's glory, are being transformed into his likeness with ever-increasing glory, which comes from the Lord, who is the Spirit."*

The disagreement between the two verses above is because the Greek verb the NASB translates "beholding as in a mirror," and the NIV translates "reflect," is *katoptrizomai* (#2734 *katoptri, zomai*). Checking different lexicons shows that *katoptrizomai* can mean "to see oneself in a mirror," and it can also mean "to reflect, as a mirror does." The scholars and translators, and thus the versions, are divided as to which meaning is the primary one in 2 Corinthians 3:18. Leaning toward "beholding as in a mirror" the glory of the Lord are versions such as the ASV, ESV, KJV, NAB, and NASB. Leaning toward "reflecting" the glory of the Lord are versions such as the HCSB, NET, NIV, NJB, and NRSV.

When a Greek word has two meanings, it can be very difficult to choose the "right" one for the verse. We must also remember that "all Scripture is God-breathed" (2 Tim. 3:16), and as the vocabulary of God, He could certainly have picked a different word than He did for this verse. We know He did not choose a word with two meanings just so Christians could fight about it. Either He thought that the context would lead us to the correct meaning of the word, or He felt that both meanings were important, even if one was more dominant than the other. That certainly seems to be the case here.

To fully understand what 2 Corinthians 3:18 is saying and to be able to translate and interpret it correctly, we must understand the record in Exodus 34, which is about Moses' face radiating the glory of God.

(29) "When Moses came down from Mount Sinai with the two tablets of the Testimony in his hands, he was not aware that his face was radiant because he had spoken with the LORD.

(30) When Aaron and all the Israelites saw Moses, his face was radiant, and they were afraid to come near him.

(31) But Moses called to them; so Aaron and all the leaders of the community came back to him, and he spoke to them.

(32) Afterward all the Israelites came near him, and he gave them all the commands the LORD had given him on Mount Sinai.

(33) When Moses finished speaking to them, he put a veil over his face.

(34) But whenever he entered the LORD's presence to speak with him, he removed the veil until he came out. And when he came out and told the Israelites what he had been commanded,

(35) they saw that his face was radiant. Then Moses would put the veil back over his face until he went in to speak with the LORD."

The record of Exodus 34:29–35 and Moses' face radiating occurred on Moses' seventh time coming down Mount Sinai from being with God and was the second time God had written the Ten Commandments on stone tablets. Exodus 34:29 tells us that Moses' face was radiant. The Hebrew text says that Moses' face shined. Moses' face was reflecting the brilliant light of God, and it was shining so brightly that the Israelites, including Aaron the High Priest, were afraid of him (34:30), and he had to cover his face with a veil (34:33,35). The illustration of Moses' face shining forth the light of God is developed in 2 Corinthian 3:7–16, which gives us many details about it.

When it comes to making a choice as to whether *katoptrizomai* means "beholding as in a mirror" or "reflecting," it seems natural that 2 Corinthians 3:18 would follow the example of Moses that is being given in the chapter. This means it would refer to our "reflecting" the glory of the Lord for others to see just as Moses radiated the glory of God for the Israelites to see.

It is not clear how "looking at oneself in a mirror" is relevant to Moses or us. Moses certainly did not see himself in any kind of mirror, he looked at God. Similarly, we do not have any glory on our own, so there does not seem to be any reason to look at ourselves in a mirror. The only reason that "beholding as in a mirror" would fit this verse in any meaningful way is that no one can reflect something he is not looking at first.

A mirror cannot reflect sunlight into a dark room unless it is pointed at the sun; "looking at" the sun if you will. When a mirror "looks at" the sun, the light is reflected off of it out to others. Similarly, we will never reflect the glory of the Lord unless we look at it. So, there is a sense in which "looking at" is a sub-theme of 2 Corinthians 3:18.

Having pointed out that Moses' face shone so brightly with the glory of the Lord that the people were afraid, we must also notice that Exodus 34:29 says that Moses' face shined "because he had spoken with the LORD." Thus, it is part of the record in Exodus that the only reason Moses could radiate the glory of the LORD to others was because he had seen it himself, and thus it makes sense that the Greek text of 2 Corinthians 3:18 would contain the subtheme of looking at the glory of the Lord as well as the theme of reflecting the glory of the Lord.

Once we understand that the concept of reflecting the glory of the Lord in 2 Corinthians 3:18 comes from the example of Moses recorded in Exodus 34, we need to pay attention to the differences and similarities between Exodus and 2 Corinthians. There are distinct differences between the record in Exodus and the record in Corinthians, and God is teaching us wonderful lessons in both places.

One of the major differences between the record in Exodus and 2 Corinthians is that in Exodus, Moses spoke directly with God and the people saw the glory reflected on Moses' face. However, Moses was a fallen human and the glory that he radiated was not permanent; it faded away (2 Cor. 3:7, 11, 13).

We all understand that at one time or another, each of us has been profoundly affected by something. We have perhaps even said, "I will never forget that" or felt like the emotion of the moment would never leave; but we do forget and emotions pass. The Israelites only saw the glory on Moses' face for a little while, and then it was gone. Moses could not hold it forever.

Today, the glory of God is not found on Moses' face, but in Jesus Christ and on his face (2 Cor. 3:14, 16, 18, and 4:6), and that glory is permanent (2 Cor. 3:11). We can always see the glory on the face of Jesus, and can always be lightened, empowered, and transformed by it.

A similarity between Exodus and Corinthians is that in Exodus, the glory of God shone from Moses' face, while today the glory is spoken of as being in the Lord, and specifically on his face. This is why 2 Corinthians speaks of "the glory of God in the face of Jesus Christ."

2 Corinthians 4:6 BSB *"For God, who said, "Let light shine out of darkness," made his light shine in our hearts to give us the light of the knowledge of the glory of God in the face of Jesus Christ."*

This verse needs to be understood in light of its context, which is chapter 3. There are times when the chapter divisions that have been added to the Bible do not help people understand it. Most people just assume that new chapters start with new subjects, and chapter 4 is a new subject from chapter 3. In this case, however, the glory of God was on the face of Moses in chapter 3, and it is on the face of Jesus in chapter 4. The glory faded from Moses' face but will never fade from Jesus' face.

There is a biblical custom about the "face" that is helpful to understand. In the biblical culture, the word "face" indicates intimacy and a connection. The glory that was on Moses' face was a physical reality, surely, but it is meaningful that Moses' whole body did not shine.

We have all seen Christians whom the Bible would refer to as "carnal" Christians. They focus their lives on worldly things and do not have much time for God, and their lives (and usually their faces) show it. They do not reflect the glory of God and are not transformed into Christ's glowing appearance. It is God's desire for us that we are all "face-to-face" with Jesus, in full fellowship with him, giving our lives to him, and reflecting his glory for all the world to see. That kind of intimate participation in the things of Christ is a choice, and we all can make it.

When it comes to reflecting the light of God as we look on the face of Jesus Christ, God created a wonderful object lesson for us: the moon. God often teaches us through nature, which is why he tells us to "go to the ant" (Prov. 6:6), or why He used the ox and donkey to reprove Israel (Isa. 1:3). The moon rules the night sky, and when there is a full moon, it shines so brilliantly that it is easy to see outside. The full moon is so bright that objects cast a distinct shadow in its light.

However, that is not the case if there is a lunar eclipse. A lunar eclipse occurs when the Earth gets between the sun and the moon. In those times, the moon was a full moon, but it looked very different from the normal monthly full moon. We can still see it but with some difficulty.

It is dark and has red overtones. It seems ominous and gloomy. What is the difference between the brilliantly white full moon and the dark and gloomy moon of the lunar eclipse? The brilliantly lit full moon is "looking at" the sun and reflecting its light. In sharp contrast, the full moon in eclipse is "looking at" the earth, and it seems to reflect all the darkness, anger, and gloom of the earth.

The difference between a regular full moon and the full moon of a lunar eclipse is a wonderful lesson. Just like the moon, if we look at the sun (oops, Son), and focus our gaze on him, we will reflect his light. We will shine brightly, and the light we reflect will be a blessing to ourselves and others. If, on the other hand, we look at the earth and focus our lives on earthly things, we will be just like the moon—our lives will be dark and ominous, angry, and depressed.

We each have the opportunity to be "transformed into his likeness with ever-increasing glory." Day after day as we fellowship with, and focus on, the things of God, we will shine brighter and brighter, and there will indeed be "ever-increasing glory."

At the end of each day, every one of us can think back over the day and see whether we have decided to fellowship with Christ and give ourselves to him or not. If we do, we will shine brighter and brighter. The world is a dark place and people need the light of Christ to shine into their lives. If we focus on Christ, we can be that light.

CHAPTER EIGHT: THE LOOKING GLASS

James 1:23–25 NASB *"For if any be a hearer of the word, and not a doer, he is like unto a man beholding his natural face in a glass: for he beholdeth himself, and goeth his way, and straightway forgetteth what manner of man he was. But whoso looketh into the perfect law of liberty, and continueth therein, he being not a forgetful hearer, but a doer of the work, this man shall be blessed in his deed."*

Two things are very obvious in the text: the first is the hearer of the Word who does not profit by it and is represented as looking into a glass. Secondly, we see the man who does profit by the Word, for he is represented as looking into the perfect law. May the Holy Spirit help us to see these clearly!

Looking into a glass is a trivial business. In all ages, men, not to say women, have been fond of seeing themselves. In the earlier days, they had no reflecting glasses as we now have, but they used mirrors made of brass and kindred metals, highly polished. These mirrors yielded a sufficiently clear image of the beholder.

Albeit, the children of Israel came out of Egypt in a great hurry, yet we find that the women carried their looking glasses with them into the wilderness. It was according to their womanly nature: whatever else they forgot, they must have the indispensable looking glass, for their toilet. It is to their praise, however, that in the desert their devotion overcame their vanity. When the brazen laver was to be made in which the priests should wash, it was made of the looking glasses of the serving women who were accustomed to meeting at the door of the tabernacle.

Still, the use of the mirror must be ranked among the trifles of life: I see that you are half-smiling at the playfulness that glitters around a glass. Is not this a hint at the light in which many regard the hearing of the gospel? They crowd to hear a preacher if he has some sort of name. Not that they desire to get a blessing, but merely that they may say that they have heard him, or that they may gratify their curiosity by seeing what he is like.

Let me say, that to every hearer, the true Word of God is as a mirror. Certain preachers dream that it is their business to paint pretty pictures: but it is not so. We are not to design and sketch, but simply to give the reflection of truth. We are to hold up the mirror to nature in a moral and spiritual sense, and let men see themselves therein. We have not even to make the mirror, but only to hold it up. The thoughts of God, and not our thoughts, are to be set before our hearers' minds; and these discover a man to himself. The Word of the Lord is a revealer of secrets: it shows a man his life, his thoughts, his heart, and his inmost self.

A large proportion of hearers only look upon the surface of the gospel, and upon their minds, the surface alone is operative. Yet even that surface is sufficiently effectual to reflect the natural face that looks upon it, and this may be of lasting service if rightly followed up.

The chief blessing cannot come to us by surface work; he that would be enriched by the gospel must dig for it and must dig deep. He must sink shafts into its fathomless mines that he may bring up "the much fine gold." Let not our thoughts glide over the surface of the Word like swift birds that touch the crests of the waves but let us plunge into the depths of Scripture like pearl-fishers who seek for hid treasures.

The Scripture gives a truthful reflection of man's nature, it lets the man see himself. Not as others see him, for others make mistakes, nor as he would see himself, for he is very apt to be partial to his soul; but the Scripture makes him see himself as God sees him.

The Holy Book does not flatter human nature, neither does the true preacher attempt to base a work; but in plain and downright honesty of truth, the witness is given. When conscience is aroused, and the man sees himself as the revelation of God declares him to be, he can hardly think that this can be the same self with which he was upon such excellent terms. If God blesses the sight, he is led to abhor himself and to seek for cleansing and renewal. But if not, the man has at least seen himself and has had the opportunity of knowing his true state.

The reflection of self in the Word is very like life. You have, perhaps, seen a dog so astonished at his image in the glass that he has barked fiercely at himself. A parrot will mistake its reflection for a rival. Under a true preacher, men are often so thoroughly unearthed and laid bare, that even the details of their lives are reported. Not only is the portrait drawn to life, but it is a living portrait that is given in the mirror of the Word. There is little need to point with the finger and say, "Thou art the man," for the hearer perceives of his own accord that he is spoken of.

As the image in the glass moves and alters its countenance, and changes its appearance, so does the Word of the Lord set forth man in his many phases, moods, and conditions. The Scripture of truth knows all about him, and it tells him what it knows.

The glass of the Word is not like our ordinary looking glass, which merely shows us our external features. According to the Greek of our text, the man sees in it "the face of his birth;" that is, the face of his nature. He that reads and hears the Word may see not only his actions there, but his motives, his desires, and his inward condition. As the butcher cuts down the carcass, and reveals all the inwards, which never could have been seen but for his knife, so is the Word of God "quick and powerful, and sharper than any two-edged sword, piercing even to the dividing asunder of soul and spirit, and of the joints and marrow, and is a discerner of the thoughts and intents of the heart."

The secrets of the man are opened up to himself, and he is astonished to see his inward depravity, his carnal tendencies, and his corrupt inclinations. As a man sees his outward self in the looking glass, so may he see his inward self in the Word; but if this be all, to what purpose is it?

Secondly, many a hearer does see himself in the mirror of the Word. We are told so twice in the text: "He is like a man beholding his natural face in a glass, for he beholdeth himself." He really does see himself, for he cannot help doing so. He is not such a careless hearer as to be utterly blind to the revelation of God: he beholds, he beholds himself, and he beholds the face of his birth. He is thoughtful during the discourse; he spies out the application of the truth to himself and marks his spots and blemishes.

Oftentimes he sees himself so plainly that he grows astonished at what he sees. He cries, like the woman of Samaria, — "Come, see a man that told me all things that ever I did." Barbarous people, when they first see looking glasses, are quite taken aback. "How can these things be?" is their first question. Now, have not you, dear hearers, who are unconverted, been often staggered at the home thrusts of the Word? You have seen yourselves so unmistakably that you have been unable to escape from the truth but have been filled with wonder at it. But what is the use of this if it goes no further?

Many of our hearers go somewhat further, for they are driven to make solemn resolves after looking at themselves. Yes, they will break off their sins by righteousness; they will repent; they will believe in the Lord Jesus; and yet their fine resolves are blown away like smoke and come to nothing. The sight of their natural face leads to a natural resolve, but the strength of nature suffices not to carry the resolution into practice.

But what follows? Observe, "He beholdeth himself, and goeth his way." Many hearers go away from what they have seen in the Word. There are two "ands" in the text, following quickly one after the other, and they have a force that I cannot very well convey to you. They show that the man looks at himself hurriedly, and as it were in passing, goes his way, and forgets what manner of man he was. This is because his glance was hasty, casual, and soon over. He heard the Word, and there was an end to it; no echoes lingered in his soul. The sermon was over when it was over.

Many a man, having seen himself in the glass of the Word, has no time for any further thought about himself. Tomorrow morning, he will be overhead and ears in business; the shutters will be down from his shop windows, but they will be put up to the windows of his soul. His office needs him, and therefore his prayer closet cannot have him; his ledger falls like an avalanche over his Bible. The man has no time to seek the true riches; passing trifles monopolize his mind.

Others have no particular business to engross them but having seen themselves in the glass of the Word with some degree of interest, they go their way to their amusements. Their principal difficulty is how to kill time and spin the weary hours away.

There are some who go their way to sin. It is not mere pleasure or business, but it is an overt act of transgression to which they go. It is an awful thing to my mind that men go from hearing the Word of God to speaking the word of the devil. They go from God's house to the house of sin; they go straight away from the holy to the profane, and from the pure to the foul. They go from the mercy seat to the seat of the scorner. I do not wonder that no good comes of such hearing as this.

When a man sees his face in the glass, and goes his way to defile that face more, of what use is the glass to him? If you return to sin, to procrastinate, and to live in wilful neglect of God and eternity, you will derive no benefit from such hearing; even if all the apostles should in turn preach to you, or even their Master himself.

This going away is followed by forgetting all they have seen. This forgetfulness is indeed very mischievous. How different is this from that

word of David, "I will never forget thy precepts"?
The wicked forget God, but the favored of the
Lord "remember his commandments to do
them." Forget the words of man but be zealous to
remember the Word of the Lord; for forgetfulness
leads to inaction.

Those who forget, forget to do. They follow
not the Lord's command in the Book of Numbers;
"Remember to do all my commandments." In
Purchas's Pilgrim, we read of certain Spaniards
of the olden times who were often pinched with
hunger, and yet immense shoals of fish passed
along their shores. They saw the fish but were too
idle to take them. Are there not many hearers of
that kind? The truth passes by them
unappropriated, unused, unpractised, and all
because they take no earnest heed to make it their
own by personal obedience to it. They say, "I go,"
but they forget to go. They see the pearl of great
price but forget to buy it. They are mere players
with the Lord's message and never come to
honest dealing with it.

Forgetfulness of the Word leads to self-
satisfaction. Looking in the glass the man felt a
little startled that he was such an ugly fellow, but
he went his way and mingled with the crowd,
and forgot what manner of man he was, and
therefore he felt quite easy again. The sweep

thinks he is as clean as his neighbors, for he has forgotten the soot upon his face.

By the force of sheer ignorance, a man can climb to a desperately false assurance of his excellence. He can cry "Peace, peace," when there is no peace, till at length a blast of trumpets will not alarm him. What can be more fatal than this? One may as well not know, as only learn, and straightway forget.

This forgetfulness leads to a growing carelessness. A man who has once looked in the glass, and afterward has not washed, is very apt to go and look in the glass again and continue in his filthiness. He who thinks his conscience has cried "wolf" in mere sport, will think the same till he takes no heed when it cries in earnest.

When men get to play with the Word of God, they are near to destruction. Beware of hearing the gospel as a pastime: it is the next stage to eternal ruin. When that which God designs to be our salvation becomes a pastime to us, then all likelihood that it will save us is gone. He who sports with heaven and hell will soon lose all hope of the one and be hurried downward to the other.

Yes, but let me remark that this forgetfulness of the Word leads to increased sin; for we do not hear the Word of God without some result coming of it.

You have seen your faces in the mirror of the Word; do you not desire to have them cleansed and beautified? You know your impurity; do you not wish to be cleansed by the blood of Jesus from all sin? Will you go your ways as if there were no law to accuse you, no gospel to invite you, and no Christ to forgive you?

The true and blessed hearer does not look into the glass, but he is represented as looking into the law: — *"Whoso looketh into the perfect law of liberty, and continueth therein, he being not a forgetful hearer, but a doer of the work, this man shall be blessed in his deed."*

The picture I have in my mind's eye at this moment is that of the cherubim upon the mercy seat: these are models for us. Their standing is upon the golden mercy seat, and our standing place is the propitiation of our Lord. There is the resting place of our feet, and, like the cherubs, we are joined thereto, and therefore continue therein.

They stand with their eyes looking downward upon the mercy seat as if they desire to look into the perfect law of God which was treasured within the ark. We look through the atonement of our Lord Jesus, which is to us as pure gold like unto transparent glass, and we behold the law, as a perfect law of liberty, in the person of our Mediator.

Like the cherubim, we are in happy company; and like them, we look towards each other, by mutual love. Our common standing is the atonement; our common study is the law in the person of Christ; and our common posture is that of angels with outstretched wings prepared to fly at the Master's bidding. Oh, that we might in this sense be as the cherubim, and like them abide in the secret place of the Most High, where the light is the light of God, and the glory is the Divine Presence!

We are not to look casually at the Word as though it were a mere looking glass; but we are to gaze earnestly upon it as our law' under the new covenant. As the apostles stooped down and looked into the sepulcher, so are we to search diligently into the blessed law of the Lord, and delight in it after the inner man.

Note well that the law of God is worth looking into. I understand by the "law" here not merely the law of Ten Commandments, but the law as it is condensed, fulfilled, and exhibited in Christ Jesus. The Gospel law, the law of the spirit of life in Christ Jesus, that gospel which we are called upon to obey, is worthy of deep meditation. I mean that holy law which the Lord has promised to put into our inward parts and write upon our hearts: the law of faith and not of self-righteousness, even the command of grace which bids us believe in the Lord Jesus Christ and obey his commands.

A law is always worth considering, for we may break the law unwittingly, and involve ourselves in penalties which we might have avoided. An unknown law is a pitfall that a man may fall into without knowing it. All loyal subjects must learn the law, so that they may obey it.

Better still, it is a perfect law. All human laws are imperfect, but the law of the Lord is perfect. The law in the hand of Christ is perfect in itself, having no excess and no deficiency; and it is a law which makes those perfect who obey it. It is a law which is outlined in the person of the perfect Christ and wrought in us by the perfect Spirit. It is a law which touches our whole nature and works it unto perfect beauty. Who would not wish to look into a law which, like its Author, is love and purity itself?

It is called the "perfect law of liberty." Now, the law under the old covenant aligns with bondage, but the law in the hand of Christ is liberty. We never walk in liberty till we walk in the Lord's commands.

The true hearer looks into this perfect law of liberty with all his soul and understanding, till he knows it, and feels the force of it in his character. He is the prince of hearers, who delights to know what God's will is and finds his joy in acting out the same. He sees the law in its height of purity, breadth of comprehensiveness, and depth of spirituality. The more he sees, the more he admires. He cannot have too much of it but meditates on it both day and night, and hence he cries, "Oh, how I love thy law! It is my meditation all the day."

His most frequent prayer is that he may be conformed unto that perfect law in all respects. In proportion as his prayer is heard, he enters into perfect rest. Now I see the meaning of that word, "We all, with open face beholding as in a glass the glory of the Lord, are changed into the same image from glory to glory, even as by the Spirit of the Lord."

A man looks into the law of liberty, and he sees all perfection in Christ. He looks until by a strange miracle of grace, his image dissolves into the image of Jesus. Surely this is a thing worth looking into, and infinitely superior to looking into a glass merely to see yourself.

He that looks into the perfect law of liberty will not only see Christ, but he will begin to see the Eternal Spirit of God bearing witness with that law of liberty and operating by that witness upon his soul. What a sight is that which lets us see the Holy Spirit working in us to will and to do of his pleasure and making us conformable to the law of his declaring! Transformation of character will follow upon meditation upon the truth of God, by the blessing of the Holy Ghost.

I have heard of a famous King of Poland, who did brave deeds in his day, and confessed that he owed his excellent character to a secret habit which he had formed. He was the son of a noble father, and he carried with him a miniature portrait of this father and often looked upon it. Whenever he went to battle, he would look upon the picture of his father, and nerve himself to valor. When he sat in the council chamber, he would secretly look upon the image of his father and behave himself. He said, "I will do nothing that can dishonor my father's name."

Now, this is the grand thing for a Christian to do: to carry about with him the will of God in his heart, and then in every action to consult that will. We ought to ask: — What shall I do, as a child of God? What course shall I follow as a man of God, bought with the precious blood of Jesus Christ? It is thought by some that you cannot continue always in the will of God. They dream that you are to hear a sermon, and then be very pious; or go to a prayer meeting, and then be very devout, but they think that this piety and devotion cannot remain with us all day.

We must continue in the law of the Lord, or we have no true religion. It is a continuous struggle for holiness. Looking at the perfect will of God is for every day and all the day. We are to believe in holiness; looking to the Lord to become like the Lord.

It is well to have Christ's portrait hung up in every chamber of your soul. I do not say of your house— that might lead to idolatry, but in every chamber of your mind and heart.

CHAPTER NINE: WHAT DO YOU SEE?

What do you see when you look in the mirror? How often do you see your reflection in a mirror? Some studies say that the average person looks in a mirror 8 to 10 times a day. Other surveys say it could be as many as 60 to 70 times a day.

Whose image do you see? What is your mirror? There are multiple mirrors in this world. Which one do you believe shows your true self: The Mirror of Social Status? The Mirror of Wealth? The Mirror of Success? The Mirror of Television? The Mirror of the Media?

We are always beholding something. What are you looking at? What are you beholding? There is a principle in the Bible that we become what we look at. Where are your eyes focused regarding who you are and your purpose in life?

A. W. Tozer said: God wants us to recognize that human nature is in a formative state and that it is being changed into the image of the thing it loves. Men and women are being molded by their affinities, shaped by their affections, and powerfully transformed by the artistry of their loves. You become what you love. You become what you chase after. In the unregenerate world of Adam, this produces day-by-day tragedies of cosmic proportions!

The eye is the critical foundation in repairing and restoring your true image. The ear is the important key to building our image to reflect how God sees us, but it all begins with the eye. The eye needs to be looking like a laser to what God says we are and that is revealed in the Bible. It is the real you and our true image.

James 1:22 *"But be ye doers of the word, and not hearers only, deceiving your own selves.*

The man who simply hears and does nothing about it is like a man catching the reflection of his face in a mirror. He sees himself, it is true, but he goes on with whatever he is doing without the slightest recollection of what sort of person he sees in the mirror. But the man who looks into the perfect mirror of God's law, the law of liberty (or freedom), and makes a habit of so doing, is not the man who sees and forgets. He puts that law into practice, and he wins true happiness.

Another translation: If some fail to do what God requires, it's as if they forget the word as soon as they hear it. One minute they look in the mirror, and the next they forget who they are and what they look like.

However, it is possible to open your eyes and take in the beautiful, perfect truth found in God's law of liberty *and live by it*. If you pursue that path and do what God has commanded, then you will avoid *the many distractions that lead to* an amnesia of all true things, and you will be blessed.

The Bible is a mirror that lets us see ourselves as God sees us.

The fundamental purpose of God's Word is to give us true self-knowledge. It is a real mirror, and when we look at ourselves properly in it, we see ourselves as God wants us to see ourselves. The assumption behind this is that the purpose of God's revelation is for us to become transformed, and to become the people God wants us to be, but this is impossible until we see ourselves as we are.

The problem with the distractions of this world is that we have amnesia, and we forget who we are. We do not have the slightest recollection of what the mirror of God's Word is showing us.

2 Corinthians 3:17–18 CSB *"Now the Lord is the Spirit, and where the Spirit of the Lord is, there is freedom. We all, with unveiled faces, are looking as in a mirror at the glory of the Lord and are being transformed into the same image from glory to glory; this is from the Lord who is the Spirit."*

Psalm 34:4–8: *"I sought the Lord, and he heard me and delivered me from all my fears. They looked unto him, and were lightened: and their faces were not ashamed. This poor man cried, and the LORD heard him, and saved him out of all his troubles. The angel of the Lord encampeth round about them that fear him, and delivereth them. O taste and see that the Lord is good: blessed is the man that trusteth in him."*

We reflect on what our eyes are focused on. Our image is determined by what we look at with our eyes and hear with our ears. Don't forget what the Word of God says about you, or the world will delude you and beat down your true identity. Our eyes are critical to our spiritual growth.

The golden rule for your life and mine is this concentrated keeping of the life open towards God. Trust Him, commune with Him, study His word, meditate, and think about it. Build it into your heart so it can tear down the strongholds of wrong images in your mind. Be passionate about your relationship with Him. Christianity is about a relationship with God. The relationship is reciprocal and mutual. No other religion claims this.

God is not a duplicator. Of the seven billion people on the planet, not one has the same fingerprint. God is not a duplicator, a copycat, and a counterfeiter. But God is a Creator, an originator, and a visionary. God only has one "you." No one can ever be "you." God only designed one "you." He only has one blueprint that he masterfully used to make a masterpiece called "you." God has designed you wonderfully unique and awesomely made as a true original. God has the most spectacular design for your life that is breathtaking and specific down to the littlest detail.

Who knows you better than God? He has loved you since the foundations of the heavens and earth. He created you. He formed you. He made you. He has had plans for you since the sun's first morning light.

Psalm 139:15–18 NLT *"You watched me as I was being formed in utter seclusion, as I was woven together in the dark of the womb. You saw me before I was born. Every day of my life was recorded in your book. Every moment was laid out before a single day had passed. How precious are your thoughts about me, O God. They cannot be numbered! I can't even count them; they outnumber the grains of sand! And when I wake up, you are still with me!"*

Jeremiah 29:11–14 ESV *"For I know the plans I have for you, declares the Lord, plans for welfare and not for evil, to give you a future and a hope. Then you will call upon me and come and pray to me, and I will hear you. You will seek me and find me, when you seek me with all your heart."*

Seek God and His plans. Know how precious you are to God. Know you have value to God. Know you have a future and a hope. It all starts by knowing your identity in Christ and seeing from Scripture who you really are.

Look at the true mirror. Behold your God! Behold His Son! Behold your salvation and birth as a son! Behold who you are!

I John 3:1–2 *"Behold what manner of love the Father hath bestowed upon us, that we should be called the sons of God: therefore the world knoweth us not, because it knew him not. Beloved, now are we the sons of God, and it doth not yet appear what we shall be: but we know that, when he shall appear, we shall be like him: for we shall see him as he is."*

Have you realized it? You are God's child, His son through the finished work of Christ.

2 Corinthians 4:4-7 ESV *"In their case the god of this world has blinded the minds of the unbelievers, to keep them from seeing the light of the gospel of the glory of Christ, who is the image of God. For what we proclaim is not ourselves, but Jesus Christ as Lord, with ourselves as your servants for Jesus' sake. For God, who said, "Let light shine out of darkness," has shone in our hearts to give the light of the knowledge of the glory of God in the face of Jesus Christ. But we have this treasure in jars of clay, to show that the surpassing power belongs to God and not to us."*

Satan, the god of this age, main goal is to blind you so you cannot see the light of the gospel, cannot see who you are in Christ, and cannot see your worth to God. God has shined in our hearts and when people see us, they should see a reflection of the glory of God.

The devil is the one who constantly throws accusations through you and about you, so you dwell on the wrong image of yourself. He is called in Scripture, the deceiver, the accuser, and the father of lies. He wants you to look in the wrong mirror and become discouraged by what you see. He wants you to think you have no worth and no value. He wants you to see sin instead of the Savior from sin.

Your value begins with the price God paid for you, which was to offer His only begotten Son, Jesus, to take your place on the cross and to suffer the torture and pain of the cross. This is so that your sin is paid in full and before the court of God, you are declared not guilty. This is unfathomable love for you. Christianity is about reconciliation, restoration, and transformation.

We are His image bearers. The fullness of God dwells in you as a Christian. The world says that you are rejected and ugly. What does the mirror say?

- The mirror says you are lovely and accepted as His beloved.
- The mirror says you are chosen.
- The mirror says all the fullness of God resides in you.
- The mirror says all your sins are forgiven.
- The mirror says you are a new creation in Christ.
- The mirror says you are justified by the blood of Christ and are at peace with God.
- The mirror says God is your heavenly Father and you are His son by the new birth.

- The mirror says you can cry "Abba Father!" to God.
- The mirror says you are blessed with all spiritual blessings in Christ.
- The mirror says you are born again and seated in heavenly places with Christ.
- The mirror says you are sealed with the Holy Spirit and have received the gift of the Holy Spirit at the time of the new birth.
- The mirror says you can energize the exceeding greatness of God's power when you believe.
- The mirror says you have been made righteous and complete in Him.
- The mirror says you are an heir of God and joint heir with Christ.
- The mirror says you have an inheritance in heaven that is undefiled and will not fade away and is reserved in heaven for you.
- The mirror says you are God's most treasured possession.
- The mirror says you are God's masterpiece.

Whether we want to admit it or not, we are pretty hard on ourselves. When we look at our reflection, we automatically say something negative about our appearance, we spit insults about how big our nose is or wish for a better body. Get this, God made that nose, He shaped that body in the way that He sees it should be. We are His creation.

No one complains about how ugly a sunset is, instead they Instagram the sunset with the hashtag #beautifulcreation. You look exactly the way you do for a purpose. If God thinks you are beautiful, then you better believe it. The same goes for inner appearance. We may not like our little quirks and wish we could be more outgoing or smarter, but we are exactly the way we are because that is the way God has always intended us to be.

Learn to love the unique person God has created you to be. If we cannot fully love ourselves then how can we fully love others? Mark 12:31 says to love your neighbor as yourself. There is not much love for other people when you are constantly bringing yourself down. How can you fulfill this command when you feel disgusted at what you see in the mirror? Take heed from the words of David in Psalms 139:14 GWT *"I will give thanks to you because I have been so amazingly and miraculously made. Your works are miraculous, and my soul is fully aware of this."*

You are miraculous. Let this sink in for a bit...you are wonderful, fantastic, and beautiful. Do not let anyone say otherwise.

In saying all of this comes a warning, excessive self-love, and vanity, is also a sin. Do not boast in your beauty because it is not of your doing. It is God's beauty, and *He* can boast in *His* creation. Honor and respect His creation, this includes yourself. Treat yourself kindly and tenderly for you would not deliberately destroy a flower for no reason. The flower and our being were crafted by the same hands, both are lovely and made whole by the almighty love of God.

The world rejects all these truths and wants you to conform to their image. The world says you are worthless and of no value. The world says you are a failure, a nobody, discarded, and abandoned. Who do you believe? What mirror are you looking at?

Romans 12:2 *"And be not conformed to this world: but be ye transformed by the renewing of your mind, that ye may prove what is that good, and acceptable, and perfect will of God."*

Do not be conformed to this world. Do not let the world squeeze you into its mold but be transformed by the renewing of your mind.

Think according to the Bible and not according to the world.

2 Timothy 3:16–17 ESV "*All Scripture is breathed out by God and profitable for teaching, for reproof, for correction, and for training in righteousness, that the man of God may be complete, equipped for every good work.*"

All Scripture is God-breathed. He only wrote one book. Its words are spiritual life. Its words vibrate with energy and power. It is an immeasurable wonder that God has given us an inspired book containing the truth about himself and his ways and what he wills for our lives.

Often, we hear that God is silent or God does not care. Don't say God is silent when your Bible is closed.

I don't know who said or shared it first, but it's clear that this simple statement resonates with many, at least it has with me. These ten words rebuke our fear that God might be inactive or uncaring in the brokenness and messiness of our lives and remind us that he cares, he sees, and he speaks. But too often, we're just not listening, and our book has remained closed.

God is always ready to speak into our lives. We simply need to listen, tuning our ears and hearts to what he is saying in the book he inspired. When we open the Bible, we find more than 750,000 words breathed out by God himself for us.

Matthew 4:4 ESV *"But he answered, "It is written, "'Man shall not live by bread alone, but by every word that comes from the mouth of God.'"*

Attention to diet is becoming more recognized as essential to nutrition and growth. A low condition of bodily health is produced by inattention to the laws of nature as to suitable diet. A low condition of spiritual health is produced by improper feeding or neglect of the necessary food, which is the Word of God. The root of all evil that abounds in the spiritual sphere at the present day lies in the fact that the Word and the words of God are not fed upon, digested, or assimilated, as they ought to be.

Our physical diet is important, but what about our spiritual diet? How much of the Word of God are we feeding upon, digesting, and assimilating into our hearts and souls? If we ever want to be spiritually strong and excel in our gifting before the Lord, we cannot neglect the spiritual food of the Bible.

Jeremiah 15:16 ESV *"Your words were found, and I ate them, and your words became to me a joy and the delight of my heart, for I am called by your name, O Lord, God of hosts."*

I Peter 2:2–3 *"As newborn babes, desire the sincere milk of the word, that ye may grow thereby: If so be ye have tasted that the Lord is gracious."*

I promise you that if you set some time aside every day to read and meditate upon the Scriptures, your life will be energized and transformed by the mighty power of His Word. There is life in the Word, and it will change the heart to become more like Him. There is light in the Word, and it will extinguish the darkness of everything that may hold us in bondage. There is comfort in the Word, and it will overcome the worries and fears of this age. There is wisdom in the Word, and it will guide our paths in the right way and help us avoid the obstacles set up to distract us and make us fall. There is healing in the Word, and it will restore our mind and body to complete wholeness.

We need to open the book and let it speak to our hearts. Pray that God enlightens your understanding and directs you to the words that you need to hear and believe. Just be faithful with being in the Word, as you will begin to realize that the more time you spend in the Word, the more you will begin to crave, desire, and cherish the time spent with God and his word. We cannot stand effectively for God without it. If we spend two minutes a week in the Word and twenty hours in front of the television, our spiritual lives will be out of balance. We will be anemic and weak spiritually, as our hearts will be receiving little nourishment from the words of God. It is like trying to put your life together without the training manual of life provided by your Heavenly Father.

People go through the journey of life looking for something useful, profitable, or advantageous for their lives. They diligently search for principles of life that will help them accomplish their goals and make their life worth living. Nothing they could ever find is more useful, beneficial, and profitable for life than the God-breathed Scriptures.

The Word of God boldly proclaims that every word contained in the Scripture is profitable. In Greek, profitable means: useful, profitable, serviceable, helpful, beneficial, and refers to that which yields advantageous returns or results. It provides something that someone needs to attain a certain goal. God has set a wonderful purpose for us in our generation, and the Word of God is the vital tool that equips us to accomplish it. The benefit and usefulness of the Bible is fathomless and so great that it cannot even be measured by human means.

A.W. Tozer said, "The Bible is not only a book which was once spoken, but a book which is now speaking." God wants to speak to us *today*, and every day, through His Word. God's word is not simply "once spoken." God's word is always "now speaking."

We silence the sound of God's voice in our lives when we leave our Bible on the shelf. Many have shared another popular statement: "Complaining about God being silent when your Bible is closed is like complaining about not getting texts when your phone is turned off."

God is always speaking to us through His Word. But the Bible is clear that we need special, God-given ears to hear him. The Scriptures call us to have "ears to hear" seven times in the Gospel, and seven more times in the beginning of Revelation. Unclog your ears from the noise of the world and listen intently to what He has to say.

Martin Luther rightly declared, "The Bible is alive, it speaks to me; it has feet, it runs after me; it has hands, it lays hold on me."

Hebrews 4:12 *"For the Word of God is quick, and powerful, and sharper than any twoedged sword, piercing even unto the dividing asunder of soul and spirit, and of the joints and marrow, and is a discerner of the thoughts and intents of the heart."*

The Word of God lives and abides forever. It cannot be destroyed, diminished, or overcome. It cannot be superseded. It will never fade or become obsolete. It is words from the heart of God, and the power of God lives in every syllable. It is the Creator of the heavens and earth, your Heavenly Father speaking. It is life-giving communication.

We all want to know who we are. We seek, search, and try to "find ourselves." Many of us have taken personality tests and other assessments. But as helpful as those tests can be, have you ever stopped to ask, "What does God think about me? Who does he say that I am?"

In all your years as a Christian, have you asked this question about who you really are? God has a lot to say about what he thinks about us—a whole Bible full. But if we could summarize it in a short space, here's how it might sound.

You Are Valuable

I am the Creator, and you are my creation. I breathed into your nostrils the breath of life (Genesis 2:7). I created you in my image (Genesis 1:27). My eyes saw your unformed substance (Psalm 139:16). I knit you together in your mother's womb (Psalm 139:13). I know the number of hairs on your head, and before a word is on your tongue, I know it (Matthew 10:30; Psalm 139:4). You are fearfully and wonderfully made (Psalm 139:14).

You are more valuable than many sparrows (Matthew 10:31). I have given you dominion over all sheep and oxen and all beasts of the field and birds of the heavens and fish of the sea (Psalm 8:6–8; Genesis 1:26, 28). I have crowned you with glory and honor as the pinnacle and final act of the six days of creation (Psalm 8:5; Genesis 1:26).

However, from the very beginning, you exchanged the truth about me for a lie. You worshiped and served created things rather than me, the Creator (Romans 1:25). You have sinned and fallen short of my glory (Romans 3:23). Just as I said to Adam and Eve, the penalty for your sin is death (Romans 6:23; Genesis 2:17). And in your sin, you were spiritually dead (Ephesians 2:1). You were children of wrath, living as enemies to me (Ephesians 2:3; Romans 5:10). You turned aside from me. You became corrupt. None does good, not even one (Psalm 14:2–3). What you deserve is my righteous judgment (Psalm 7:11–12).

Yet, in my great love, I gave my unique Son, that all those who believe in him will not perish but have everlasting life (John 3:16). While you were still sinners, Christ died for you. While you were still hostile toward me, you were reconciled to me by the death of my Son (Romans 5:8, 10). Sin doesn't have the last word. Grace does (Romans 5:20). Now everyone who calls on the name of Jesus will be saved (Romans 10:13). You who have believed are born again (1 Peter 1:3). I have adopted you (Ephesians 1:5). You are children of God, heirs of God (1 John 3:2; Romans 8:16–17). You are no longer orphans. You belong to me (John 14:18; 1 Corinthians 6:19). And I love you as a perfect Father (1 John 3:1; Luke 15:20–24).

You Are New

In my eyes, you are a brand-new creation. The old has passed away; the new has come (2

Corinthians 5:17). Sin is no longer your master, for you died to sin and are now alive to me (Romans 6:11; Ephesians 2:4–5). You are finally free from the slavery of sin and death. There is now no condemnation for you (Romans 8:1–2). All your sins are forgiven (1 John 1:9). All your unrighteousness has been cleansed by the blood of Jesus (1 John 1:7, 9). You are now righteous in my sight with the very righteousness of my perfect Son (Romans 4:5). You've been saved by grace (Ephesians 2:8). You've been justified by faith (Romans 5:1). You are utterly secure in me; nothing will be able to separate you from my love in Christ Jesus (Romans 8:39). No one can snatch you out of my hand (John 10:29). And I will never leave you nor forsake you (Hebrews 13:5).

You Have My Spirit

You not only have a new Father, but also a new family of brothers and sisters (Luke 8:21). You are now part of the people of God (1 Peter 2:9). Together, the life you now live is by faith in my Son (Galatians 2:20). Look to Jesus. Keep your eyes on him. He is the author and perfecter of your faith (Hebrews 12:2). Christ is in you by my Spirit, and you are in Christ (John 15:5; Colossians 1:27). Stay close to Jesus. Abide in him (John 15:4). For your life is found in him (John 14:6; Colossians 3:3–4). To live is Christ, and to die is gain (Philippians 1:21). Don't live by your power or understanding. No, live by my Spirit within you (Zechariah 4:6; Proverbs 3:5). Remember, I have given you the Holy Spirit to be with you and in you (Romans 5:5; John 14:17). The Spirit will guide you into all truth, help you to obey me, and empower you to do my work (John 16:7, 13; Acts 1:8; Galatians 5:16).

You Will Be Transformed

As you seek me and see more of my glory, I am transforming you into the image of my Son (2 Corinthians 3:18; Exodus 33:18). One day you will be changed, in a moment, in the twinkling of an eye, at the last trumpet shall sound (1 Corinthians 15:52). When Jesus appears, you will be like him because you shall see him as he is (1 John 3:2; Romans 8:29). You will be delivered from your body of death through Jesus Christ, and your dwelling place will be with me (Romans 7:24–25; John 14:3). I will wipe away every tear from your eyes, and death shall be no more, neither shall there be mourning, nor crying, nor pain anymore (Revelation 21:3–4). You will drink from the spring of the water of life without payment, and I will make for you a feast of rich food and well-aged wine (Revelation 21:6; Isaiah 25:6). You will enter my rest, inherit the kingdom I've prepared for you, and step into fullness of joy and pleasures forevermore (Hebrews 4:9–11; Matthew 25:34; Psalm 16:11). But most of all, you will see my face and be with me where I am (Revelation 22:4; John 14:3).

You Represent Me

Hebrews 12:2 *"Looking unto Jesus the author and finisher of our faith."*

Therefore, walk in a manner worthy of your calling (Ephesians 4:1). You are no longer darkness, but light in my Son. Walk as children of light (Ephesians 5:8). You are the light of the world, a city set on a hill (Matthew 5:14). I have called you (2 Peter 1:3). I have chosen you (Revelation 17:14). You are now a saint, a servant, a steward, and a soldier (Romans 1:7; Acts 26:16; 1 Peter 4:10; 2 Timothy 2:3). You are a witness and a worker (Acts 1:8; Ephesians 2:10). Through Jesus, you are victorious (1 Corinthians 15:57). You have a glorious future (Romans 8:18). You are a citizen of heaven (Philippians 3:20). You are an ambassador for my Son (2 Corinthians 5:20).

I have only scratched the surface of what the Bible says about you. God is very personal when it comes to you. He thinks about you all the time. He cares about you immensely. Open the book and let Him speak to you and show you who you really are!

The greatest tragedy in life is when we turn our backs on God's design and purpose for our lives. This tragedy hurts the heart of God for He knows what could have been. The story that never came to pass; the beautiful masterpiece that was left in the box; the awesome calling that faded away. He has written a beautiful story for our life, but when we pick up the pen and try to write the book ourselves, everything falls apart and crumbles before our eyes.

Pray to God. Talk to God. Ask God to show you day by day His design, function, and purpose for you on this earth. Pray to God that you fulfill every jot and tittle of it. It is glorious. It is immense. It is adventurous. It is the best.

This purpose always has at its fabric that you have a heart of service to God and others. It begins with salvation in the Lord Jesus Christ and the new birth. No one can accomplish their destiny without the Lord Jesus Christ. God is with you every step of the way and He will help you, strengthen you, and guide you into fulfilling his purpose for you in your generation. Don't ever waste your potential, your purpose, and your design on things, paths, and ways that God never intended for you. Be all that you can be for God. Every cell in your body was designed for you to fulfill your purpose which God knew about before time began. Let God make your life count and ring as a gem of God's glory throughout the halls of eternity forever. Every moment counts; everyday counts; every week counts; and every year counts, but we live with God one day at a time.

Romans 10:11 NASB *For the Scripture says, "Whoever believes in Him [whoever adheres to, trusts in, and relies on Him] will not be disappointed [in his expectations]."*

The glitter of the world with its man-made theories and philosophies will always let you down. It is like building your life on sinking sand. God will never disappoint. God will never let you down. Faith is a gateway to recovery and discovery. The truth about who you are will set you free. The Bible opens the prison door and obliterates self-condemnation and self-hatred. It enables you to love yourself because it shows you how much God loves you and what He has done for you.

It all begins with the call to salvation; the invitation of Jesus Christ to come and see. He is the Way, He is the Truth, and He is the Life. Only he has the promise of life that is in Christ for now and for all eternity. You will not thirst again when you come to him for, he is living water and holds the keys to eternal life.

I Timothy 2:3–6 ESV *"This is good, and it is pleasing in the sight of God our Savior, who desires all people to be saved and to come to the knowledge of the truth. For there is one God, and there is one mediator between God and men, the man Christ Jesus, who gave himself as a ransom for all."*

The transformation of who we are, and the restoration of our true image begins with the new birth in Christ. Repent of your past sin, turn to God, confess Jesus as your Lord, believe that God raised him from the dead, and receive the gift of eternal life and complete salvation. This is the new beginning for our lives and then we let God build us through His Word. Think of yourself as God thinks of you. No other opinion is important. Look in the mirror of the Bible, the God-breathed Word to see the real you, the one that Jesus gave his life for.

You have immense worth. You have immeasurable value. You are God's treasure put on this earth to shine as a light. Never let the world convince you otherwise. Take God's hand in this new adventure. Know that God loves you more than you will ever be able to comprehend, and He is here every moment for you. He is for you. He is your refuge. He is your strength. He is your helper. He is everything we ever need in life. He will never abandon you, never forsake you, and never leave you. Now is the time to return to your loving Heavenly Father. Now is the time to make Christ your Lord and to be set free from every bondage and every prison that holds you captive.

Numbers 6:24–26 ESV *"The Lord bless you and keep you; the Lord make his face to shine upon you and be gracious to you; the Lord lift up his countenance upon you and give you peace."*

ACKNOWLEDGMENTS

First, praises to the God Almighty and Jesus Christ for His inspirational words of wisdom throughout my writing to supply me with sufficient grace to complete this book successfully.

I would like to express my deep and sincere gratitude to my fellow pastors and mentors at Living Faith Church, Winners Chapel International, worldwide. Also, my immense gratitude to my ministry team at GLOC (www.greatestloveofchrist.com).

The dynamism, vision, sincerity, and motivation have deeply inspired me. They have taught me the principles of covenant-conscious and heaven-focused living. It was a great privilege and honor to work and serve under the guidance of my fellow ministers. I am extremely grateful for the privileges and impartation from our Bishop.

I would also like to thank our families and friends for their friendship, empathy, and great sense of humor.

I am extending my heartfelt thanks to my wife and my awesome children and family for their unrelenting support. This also includes my wonderful sister and the entire Zoba's Facilities team for their kind assistance in publishing this book. I am extremely grateful for all the love, prayers, care, and sacrifice to prepare me for my future.

Also, I express my thanks to my wonderful mother, sisters, brother, sister-in-law, and brothers-in-law for their support and valuable prayers.

AUTHOR BIO

Norman Fletcher is a contemporary, technical, and spiritual writer. He originated from the United Kingdom but recently emigrated with his family to the United States. He has been writing blogs for over six years on various subjects ranging from religion to politics and technological explorations. In the course of his master's in software engineering, he regularly made time to study history books to gain a full understanding of the Roman era and traditions.

He also loves to travel and has visited over a dozen countries across four continents (Europe, Asia, Australia, and the Americas, inclusive) where he embarks on travel writing whilst understudying the people, language, and culture that he is immersed in at the time.